in your own words

in your own words

Extraordinary tales

from

ordinary life

Edited by Anna Murphy

SIMON &
SCHUSTER

London · New York · Sydney · Toronto

A VIACOM COMPANY

The Sunday Telegraph

First published in Great Britain by Simon & Schuster UK Ltd, 2005
A Viacom company

1 3 5 7 9 10 8 6 4 2

Simon & Schuster UK Ltd
Africa House
64–78 Kingsway
London WC2B 6AH
www.simonsays.co.uk

Simon & Schuster Australia
Sydney

A CIP catalogue record for this book is available
from the British Library.

ISBN 0-7432-6814-8
EAN 9780743268141

Typeset by M Rules
Printed and bound in Great Britain by
William Clowes Ltd, Beccles, Suffolk
Lettering by Per Karlen

With thanks to the Frank Hodgson Memorial Fund, Gillingham
School, Harding's Lane, Gillingham, Dorset, SP8 4QP for permission
to include 'A gentleman and a scholar'.

To Mum and Dad, the first people to tell me stories,
and to my dear Paul

Contents

Acknowledgements

I would like to thank my colleagues at the *Sunday Telegraph Magazine* for their help with the 'In Your Own Words' column.

Introduction

What makes a story worth telling? A striking character or event. A memorable moment in time, or a place or a thing. Stories are the stuff of fiction – novels, plays, myths, fairytales – but they are also the stuff of fact: they are what make up our newspapers and television news, our history books; they are our past, our present and our future.

Increasingly in the media and in literature today, the voices of 'ordinary' people are heard. There are books by people who have suffered bereavements, there are newspaper interviews with people who have lost ten stone. There are television documentaries in which people 'swap' wives or climb mountains or live their lives on the screen for weeks on end. Yet every one of these stories has to fit a certain format, to have – as it were – a reason for being heard.

What about those other more shapeless stories that

don't get shared, stories that are all the more compelling precisely because they refuse to be typecast? What about the odd things that happen to people, the incidental things that make them laugh, or cry, or scratch their head; the stories they carry with them for the rest of their lives, and retell to their family and friends countless times over the years. There has been nowhere for them to be heard.

It was this that led to the launch of a new column, called 'In Your Own Words', in the *Sunday Telegraph Magazine* in November 2003. A weekly column, written by our readers, its brief was simple: six hundred words based on something from real life, a point at which the ordinary had turned extraordinary.

As editor, I was concerned about two things. Would we receive enough submissions? And would they be any good?

I need not have worried. The response was immediate, and enormous: hundreds of accounts from the lives of our readers. And the standard was amazingly high. Those which we printed in the magazine, and which are gathered together for the first time in this book, were altered by barely a word – something that can rarely be said for the work of many journalists!

I came to realise that these were stories that had already been polished and fine-tuned in numerous oral retellings; there was nothing left for us to do. The standard of the best of them – in literary terms alone – was remarkable: immaculate narrative pacing, linguistic precision, genuine feeling; the understanding that, so often with the written word, less is more.

What kind of stories are you about to read? What experiences in our readers' lives did they consider worth sharing with you? Many of them are, at root, the stuff of fairytale. There is a Cinderella, who finally gets to go to the RAF ball decades after the death of the beloved fiancé who was originally going to take her. There is a Scrooge who carries his fortune around with him in a battered old raincoat. There is even an accidental Jesus figure, a hitchhiker who starts to suspect that the welcoming residents in an Italian town have mistaken his arrival for that of a rather more important guest.

Are these stories recognisably British, or English? National characteristics are slippery, sometimes dangerous things. But think of it this way: would another country have produced a similar set of tales? Of course there are the geography-free experiences of human life: birth, death, love, hate. Yet a good number of these narratives are set against a peculiarly English landscape: an empty, windswept beach; a spick-and-span caravan; an old bombsite turned impromptu playground.

Many of the props are quintessentially English, too: a beloved Yorkshire terrier, an exploding rice pudding, Bridget Jones-style big knickers, a troublesome Triumph motorbike. So, too, are some of the character types: eccentrics, such as a brawny tattoo-covered thimble collector called Jock; travellers, trying to get trains in forlorn bits of India, or running from a friend's pet crocodile in Nigeria; people obsessed with their pets, or their antiques, or getting hold of a turkey for Christmas in the middle of Africa. And every so often there is a famous name – Kim Philby, Quentin Crisp –

popping up briefly, but unforgettably, in the middle of someone else's more anonymous existence.

Above all, these are stories recounted by narrators whose eye for detail, whose sense of what is funny or sad, or simply worth noting, is remarkably akin to our own. We recognise these narrators; and they, in turn, would recognise us.

Countless readers of the *Sunday Telegraph* have contacted the magazine over the last two years to tell us how much they love the 'In Your Own Words' column; how it is the first thing they turn to every Sunday. Sometimes the letters have been affectingly precise. For example we ran a story by a woman who in 1948 went to the French village where Paul, the man she was going to marry, had been shot down during the war. A letter came into the office from someone in the village who remembered, as a little girl, making the wreath that lay on Paul's coffin.

Some of the stories in this book will move you, some will make you laugh; all of them will make you ponder a little and take stock. The fact is that we all love to know about other people, especially ordinary people, people 'like us'. After all, how, as a child, do we learn to live? By observing the lives of those close to us, by listening to their account of the world. The human condition is essentially one of nosiness; the moment we lose interest in the narratives of the world around us, we lose interest in life itself. Reading someone else's story – hearing what they have to say 'in their own words' – ultimately helps us to make sense of our own.

Anna Murphy

Childhood Memories

A gentleman and a scholar

On an afternoon in July 1963 I was walking through the corridors of my comprehensive school in Gillingham, Dorset, saying goodbye to the few teachers I had liked. Then I knocked on the door of Frank Hodgson's physics classroom and my life changed for ever. I had just taken my O-levels. I was sixteen and it was time I got a job. Our household was painfully poor. My father was in prison, halfway through a three-year stretch for running a fraudulent horserace betting scheme. Unsupported by state benefits, my mother was earning £8–£10 a week working in a piston-ring factory. Our rent on an unfurnished flat in central Salisbury with a bath in the kitchen and an inspiring, elevating view of the back of the cathedral was £4 a week. The £2–£3 a week that I could earn washing-up in the County Hotel or selling clothes at Salisbury market were not enough. Warning me that I would hate the work and that it had ruined his own life, the librarian at Salisbury City Library offered me a full-time job at £5 a week. My mother and I talked it over but there was no doubt about the decision: I had to leave school.

When I knocked on the door of his classroom, Frank Hodgson came out into the corridor to talk to me.

'I came to say goodbye because I'm leaving today,' I said.

'No, you're not,' he answered, sternly. 'I won't let you.'

'Yes, I am,' I said, laughing at the notion that he might have the power to stop me. 'I've got a job.'

'Look,' he said, unsmiling, 'I can't talk about this now because I've got a class to teach but come back at the end of this period and we'll sort this out. I am determined that you must stay on into the sixth form and give yourself a chance of getting to university.'

When I went back, I told Frank about the job at the library.

'What's the pay?' he asked.

'Five pounds a week.'

'Right,' he said, immediately. 'If it will keep you at school, I will give your mother five pounds a week until your father comes out of prison.'

The full financial measure of this flabbergasting offer did not strike me until I was the sole supporter of a family of my own – as Frank was then. He would have been earning about £40 a week; £5 was roughly 15 per cent of his take-home pay. Would any teacher with a family be willing or able to make such a sacrifice today? With the blessing of the City librarian who said I was better off out of it, I went back to

4

Gillingham in September 1963 to start the sixth form and a period I regard as one of the happiest of my life. I mopped up a hatful of A*- and A-levels, was made head boy and, in June 1965, was offered an unconditional place at Cambridge.

A few days before my father came home from prison, my mother gave me an envelope to deliver to Frank Hodgson. When I gave Frank the envelope, he looked into the mass of banknotes with amazement. 'I've never saved this much money in my life,' he said, chortling. It contained all the money he had given my mother. She hadn't spent a penny. She had kept me at school through her own efforts.

Alex Barnacle

Bad hair day

I must have been around fourteen years old when my mother summoned me to the bathroom. 'You have to help me,' she said. 'I'm trying to get your father's hair back to how it used to be.'

Thinning a little on top and decidedly mousy brown with a few streaks of grey, my father, it seemed, was but a shadow of his former self. It wasn't the first time she'd mentioned his lack of lustrous blond hair. She'd tell everyone who would listen what a gorgeous blond he was when she'd first met him. He'd been captain of both the local cricket and rugby teams, soaring through grammar school in the 50s, and on to university. She'd been so proud. I suppose that's how she had eventually cajoled him into the bathroom for a spot of peroxide treatment. He had an important conference to attend the following day and going blond again was to, well, give him an edge – get him noticed.

Dutifully I helped her apply the mixture as directed on the packet. Patiently we wrapped his hair in clingfilm, placed a towel around his shoulders and waited for the transformation. Well, we chatted over his head about this and that for a while, until it could be avoided no longer – he was turning chicken yellow before our horrified eyes. Quickly my mother ran a bowl of hot water and shoved his head under.

'Anything wrong?' my dad enquired as he gasped for air.

'No, nothing at all,' my mother replied hysterically, shoving his head under again. 'Sarah, go and get the Vim,' she shrieked.

By this time I was giggling uncontrollably, unable to meet my mother's eye. We scrubbed and scrubbed until his poor scalp was raw, but nothing would shift the bright yellow dye. Eventually we had to concede that damage limitation was the only option. I got the scissors.

'Are you sure there's nothing wrong?' Dad asked again.

'No, absolutely nothing,' my mother told him in between spurts of laughter. 'Now sit there and let Sarah cut and dry it.'

I then cut his hair in the fashion of the day – a sort of Rod Hull pudding-bowl cut which I carefully blow-dried under all the way round. Mum and I tried desperately to stifle our rising hysteria as Dad, without looking in the mirror, donned the burgundy velvet jacket that my mother had just bought him from Marks & Spencer's, and left to go and pick my younger brother up from a party. He looked like a character from *Hamlet*. I only learned later that my 12-year-old brother had taken one look at his father through the window of his friend's house and refused to open the door. I think that was when Dad finally twigged.

He gave his lecture the next day dressed in a suit and deerstalker.

Sarah England

Out of the ashes

I was about ten years old when the three-day week started in the early 1970s. There were endless power cuts and the electricity to homes, street lighting and non-essential businesses was often simply cut off.

At our house in Motherwell, in the shadow of the Ravenscraig steelworks, we had a coal fire, as did most of our neighbours. Like them we could rarely afford to buy enough fuel to last all week, so everything in the house that could be burnt and was not essential would end up on the fire.

Much to my grief, during the worst weeks of the cuts the oil paintings by my stepfather, Joe, who worked at the steelworks, found their way on to the fire. Joe was always the one to select the painting to be sacrificed and he would be the one who, without any visible emotion, would snap it over his knee and place it on top of the bundles of rolled up paper and splinters of wood.

With no radio or television, and without sufficient light to read by, the entire family would usually go to bed in the early evening – our beds had been moved into the living-room as it was the only room with a fireplace. To begin with, these evenings were a bit of an adventure for us children. The two oldest would tell ghost stories while I, the youngest, would cling to my mother in fear. But my parents, exhausted by the struggles of everyday life, just wanted to get to sleep; chatting was discouraged.

It was on one such evening that Joe put the last of his paintings on the fire. I had hoped that things would improve and this painting would not have to be burnt. It was my favourite. In my childish self-absorption it never occurred to me to think how it must have affected Joe. The painting was of his oldest son as a toddler and he had no photographs of him at that age. I was determined to watch every inch of the painting succumb to the flames. As the rest of my family slept, I watched the yellow and red of the boy's checked trousers mingle and melt into the rough side of the cheap hardboard which Joe had used as a canvas.

As I looked up from the flames I saw the dark outline of a man. I caught sight of him picking up the clock and ornaments from our mantelpiece and putting them into his coat. I let out a cry and my parents awoke to see a close neighbour of ours standing among us, stealing from us. Joe calmly told the man to put the things back and get out.

The next day, the incident was not mentioned. When

the man passed my parents in the street, they exchanged a salutatory nod as they always had. My parents despised dishonesty but this man had been made redundant from the steelworks several years earlier and was struggling to bring up two small sons alone. They had decided that he had been desperate and to take action against him (legal or otherwise) would only hurt the sons he loved.

Eventually electricity supplies, and life in general, returned to normal but Joe never picked up a paintbrush again. Although in earlier times some paintings had been given to friends and neighbours who had admired them, to my knowledge none has survived.

Arlene Hassan

Hunger strike

As the tram rattled along the road, the air-raid siren sounded. Up and down, up and down, it wailed. However many times I heard it, my stomach always lurched in trepidation. The passengers on the tram appeared nonchalant. But it was only a pretence, masking unknown fears. Everyone was apprehensive of what might happen as the air raid progressed.

We didn't have to wait long. In the distance, ominously, we heard the sound of a V1 bomb. It stopped abruptly. Silence. Then it delivered its lethal cargo, an unwanted donation from Germany.

All the passengers instinctively crouched on the floor. The ensuing explosion shook the tram from side to side, and we were thrown in heaps together. Looking round to see that no one was hurt, we scrambled off the tram, filled with alarm and confusion, dreading what damage we would see.

The bomb had fallen 200 yards away.

I realised quickly that it had exploded near to where I lived. My only thought was to get home. I ran and ran. I could hardly breathe with the extra exertion and a sharp restricting pain in my chest. On the way to the dreadful scene, ambulances and fire engines passed me by. My mind seemed numb as I ran. I willed it to be empty of any thoughts about what I might find.

I passed a street raging with fires. Hardly a house was left standing, where minutes before it had been an ordinary suburban scene. Now it was flattened. Later I was told that the children playing in the street, as well as the parents in their homes, were all killed.

As I came to the top of the road where I lived I could see that although the houses were badly damaged, they were not completely demolished. Rooftops had been ripped off by the blast, and complete rooms were opened up, with all the furniture showing, like a doll's house. I picked my way down the road through the rubble, searching for some familiar object or person, avoiding the bodies on stretchers, not looking too closely at faces – fearful of recognising someone I might know.

I was very frightened. Then I saw my parents, in front of what was once our home. They stood, barely recognisable, covered from head to foot in soot. But unhurt.

'Thank God you're all right,' my mother said. 'You're all right, dear. You're all right,' she repeated.

'Yes,' I said. 'I'm all right. But what about you?'

She ignored my question, and said, 'You haven't had any dinner. It's in the oven!'

'Oh, Mum, I don't want any dinner. How can I eat, seeing all this?'

An air-raid warden came by and, seeing my mother so upset, said, 'What's the matter, ducks?'

Mum said, 'My daughter has just come home from work, and she hasn't had any dinner. It's still in the oven . . .'

'Just a minute,' the man said. Straight away he clambered over what was once our steps, through where there had once been a door. A few minutes later he reappeared with a plate recovered from the smashed oven. The dish was full of food, covered in pieces of brick and dust.

'Here you are, love,' he said, handing me the plate. 'There's your dinner!'

Looking at it, we all laughed, happy to be alive.

Joy Miles

Down the drain

When I was seven, we – that is, my father, my mother, my 4-year-old sister and I – lived in Changi, Singapore, not far from the infamous jail. In those days, nearly fifty years ago, the streets were noisy and colourful places – assorted washing was hung out on bamboo poles from overhead windows and radios playing Chinese music vied with each other from open-fronted shops. Chinese, Malays and Indians, as well as Europeans like ourselves, milled about in the damp heat, shopping, shouting, eating and spitting – sometimes on the pavement, but often in the road, dodging hooting cars and an endless stream of aged black bicycles. Skinny dogs and pathetic-looking cats added to the jumble of life. But quite apart from the colours and the noise was the smell – an indescribable mixture of competing cuisines, sweat, sewers and household refuse.

It was in just such a street that an awful event occurred which, to this day, I have never been allowed to forget.

For some reason which now escapes me, my sister and I had been dressed in fresh cotton dresses normally kept for church and tea-parties. We had been given a letter to post, each of us holding a corner and both of us slightly pulling at it as we ran towards the letterbox. I was determined that it should be me that put the letter into the hole, so, at the last minute, I gave my sister an almighty shove.

The letter went into the box right enough, but, to my horror, my sister lost her balance and keeled over into a deep open storm drain. When I looked over, she was bobbing about in the filthy grey water, her blue dress with rabbits around the hem billowing up behind her like an inflatable buoyancy aid. She was doing doggy-paddle and my mother was hanging over the edge, telling her to keep her head up.

There was a huge commotion – especially from the Chinese who had been sitting in a nearby open-air restaurant. Eventually they managed to lean over and haul my sister out, soaking wet, stinking and crying.

My mother was beside herself with rage. The only words that I actually remember were, 'If that child dies of typhoid or dysentery, it'll be all your fault.'

I thought my sister would most certainly die. But there was nothing I could say. The fault was entirely mine and mine alone.

All the way home in the back of a taxi, wrapped in a towel and still stinking of drains, my sister wailed. No one spoke to me, except my mother, who constantly reminded me that I was responsible for my sister's imminent death.

When we eventually got home, she was put straight into a bath of Dettol. I remember seeing her sitting there in the white water, smelling of disinfectant, and having her hair washed by my mother in rubber gloves. And I remember thinking that perhaps, if I was lucky, she might pull through after all.

Well, she did.

But I still can't look at a bottle of Dettol, with its familiar sword logo, without recalling this hideous incident. And when we all get together at Christmas, when the meal is over and conversation turns to family memories, I just know that before the afternoon is out my sister will ask, 'Do you remember the time you pushed me in the drain?' And our now grown-up children will roar with laughter.

Frances Welby

Oven ready

The Black Hand Gang were all local lads. 10-year-old boys with a tough and pugnacious leader nicknamed Acker. I longed to join this intrepid, elite group. They balanced on railway bridge parapets (much to the wrath of alarmed engine drivers), had a hideaway of bracken in the bluebell wood, and always sat in the third row of the stalls for Saturday matinées at the local cinema. One Friday evening I found them at the bottom of the lane leaning up against the warm brick wall of the village bakery. My knees were knocking, but it was now-or-never-time: 'I want to join your gang.'

Acker spat in the dry clay dust below his clogged feet. 'No chance.'

'Why not?'

'Simple. You're a girl. We don't have girls in the Black Hand Gang.'

'You ought to. I'm tough. I can do anything you boys can.'

Acker sniggered but said nothing.

'Yes, I can. Give me something to prove it. I'll do it.'

There was a long silence. Acker spat again.

The gob landed at my feet. 'Hop it. Come back tomorrow and we'll think something up.' I could hear them laugh as I walked away. Next day was a torment. I just couldn't settle to do any work at school. I was thinking hard what tricks the Black Handers might have up their sleeves for a soppy girl and wondering how I could prove that I would be a worthy member of the gang.

The group of six lads fell silent when I approached that evening.

'What do you want me to do, then?'

'If you can go into the bakery and get in the bread oven and stay in it for five minutes, you can be the first girl in our gang.'

I was willing to do anything to be a Black Hander. We walked through the stable past Samson, the baker's horse. The new straw smelled sweet and the horse whinnied as we passed him. The bakehouse door was unlocked. It was always left open – we lived in a law-abiding village.

Inside the bakehouse it was deathly quiet. The sun was setting over the Bristol Channel and little fingers of red, dying light glowed through dusty cracked windowpanes. The air smelled close and heavy like the bottom of old grain sacks, and the floor was coated with grey flour dust. Our silent feet left prints as we walked. Acker stopped at what seemed like a big metal cupboard and opened the very heavy door. The interior stretched into a black void.

'If you want to join the gang, you'll have to get in there. We'll shut the door on you and come back to get you out in five minutes.'

'Right,' I said, but my voice was quaking and my legs were shaky.

I scrambled in head first and the thick black iron door clanged shut. Everything was suddenly black and noiseless. I was shut off completely from the world. Incarcerated in a warm, metal coffin and, apart from the gang, no one knew where I was. Possibly they had all gone home and left me there. In the morning Mr Scribbins would light up the big wood oven and I would be slowly roasted to death. I lay in complete terror, traumatised, choking on old flour dust in that scary, dark chamber.

After what seemed like hours the door opened and Acker pulled me out by my feet.

I coughed and spluttered as I emerged, my eyes running and my heart beating nineteen to the dozen. 'You can be a member of our gang,' he said matter-of-factly. 'See you at the cinema on Saturday afternoon. Don't forget, third row of the stalls.'

The gang moved off and didn't wait for me. I stopped to pat Samson as I walked through his stable. Tears were pouring down my flour-caked face as I threw up into a pile of hay.

Pam Clatworthy

Peep show

It was a hot summer afternoon towards the end of the school holidays and we two eight-year-olds set off to enjoy it at our favourite spot – the Gorse Field. This was rough pastureland running from the old farmhouse down a steep slope to the brook in the valley. It was a poor field full of thistles, where occasionally there would be cows or horses. At the bottom of the hill was a ring of gorse bushes tucked away at one side (hence its name). It was a real hidey-hole for imaginative little girls. We hurried to the gap in the gorse and stopped; someone was there. A couple lay half-hidden in the little grassy hollow towards the middle of the ring. There appeared to be a pile of shoes nearby and a pair of striped trousers laid out on the grass with the white braces catching the sunlight. We sat down.

The couple were making a lot of animal noises. The man

was sort of lying on top of the girl with his bare bottom showing and his sock-clad feet, suspenders still intact, digging frantically into the ground. We couldn't see much of the girl, just a bent bare leg and a pair of hands grabbing round the man's neck. Her bright red nails looked like a lot of little beetles across the man's shoulders. We watched fascinated. So that's how it was done. I knew all about the making of babies but had never quite worked out the mechanics of it all.

The grunting got louder and the movements faster; then suddenly they stopped and the man rolled off on to his side with his back to us. The girl sat up. She had a long page-boy hairstyle, which was in a bit of a mess. Her blouse was open and she didn't seem to have a bra on, as you could see her breasts. The man reached up and squeezed one. She laughed and bent over and kissed him. When she straightened up again, she saw us, pointed and screamed. Startled, we shot to our feet. The man turned and seemed to explode. 'You little buggers,' he bellowed, 'I'll kill you.' His face was red with anger and, as he got to his feet, he looked like a giant.

Terrified, we started to run back up the hill as fast as we could. We heard the man panting and shouting behind us. It seemed to go on forever, and the hill had never been steeper. Then suddenly, he let out a yelp as if he was in pain and started swearing.

We stopped to look back. The man was hopping about on one leg trying to rub his other foot – he'd trodden on a thistle. We began climbing again, slower now and moving backwards, watching. The man shook his fist at us and shouted something, then to our relief, stumbled off back down the hill towards the gorse. He looked really comical with his bare legs and his shirt-tail flapping, and several times he nearly fell over. We watched for a few seconds, and then headed for home. We were pretty silent on the way back. We never talked about what we had seen, then or later. Nor did we tell anybody else about it. And we never went to play in the Gorse Field again.

Barbara Richards

A real sweetie

About the time I was ten I took to visiting my grandparents every Sunday morning. This was a real treat for me as I was very fond of both of them. I also enjoyed the weekly visit to their local shop. The order was always the same: a copy of the *News of the World* and a quarter of Quality Street. Buying Quality Street loose was an adventure. I knew all the varieties and the colour of wrapper each was contained in, but which ones came out of the jar was purely a matter of chance. I had my two absolute favourites – praline and orange cream. On the way back to Nan and Granddad's I could never resist opening the tightly twirled bag to view its contents. My mouth watered instantly if I spotted a pink-wrapped oblong praline or a soft-centred, tangy orange cream. Alas, I have to confess my greed always got the better of me. I reckoned just one sweet would not be missed.

Because I was always given first choice of a sweet as my reward, I had a strict order of misappropriation. I took one of my favourites if there was more than one. If only one, I would save that for my 'reward' and settle instead for a hard, chocolate-covered toffee. I would suck off the chocolate slowly and then resist chewing the toffee to make it last as long as possible. Sometimes I could make it last all the way back to my grandparents' gate.

My deception continued unashamedly. Then the weekly Quality Street lottery dealt a retaliatory hand. One Sunday, on opening the bag, nearly every sweet turned out to be either a praline or an orange cream. I thought I'd died and gone to chocolate heaven.

An orange cream was quickly devoured. Too quickly. Temptation proved too strong for a post-war, sweet-starved ten-year-old. A praline disappeared next, then another orange cream. The bag became worryingly light. By the time I handed it over there were only two ounces left. I wasn't offered my usual sweet. Nan and Granddad talked in low voices. I looked on fearfully, sure I was 'for it'. Instead Nan got out her kitchen scales and the bag was ceremoniously weighed. Granddad then took out a little red book and noted down the figures.

I could see he had a long list of dates and weights. Every one of my transgressions had been dutifully recorded. I was struck dumb with shame.

Neither Nan nor Granddad spoke a word. Granddad went into the hall and put on his coat: 'I'm going to have it out with that thieving shopkeeper right now. Taking advantage of a young girl.'

It suddenly hit me: I was not suspected. They thought the shopkeeper had been giving me short measure each week. Now I really was ashamed.

Suitably chastened I returned home. The following Sunday I visited as normal. It would have been odd not to. The usual was said. 'A *News of the World* and a quarter of Quality Street, please.' I waited till the shop was busy, and went in asking for my order in as innocent a voice as I could muster. The shopkeeper treated me with his usual indifference. The order was filled, but the thrill had gone. A full quarter was handed over to Nan and Granddad. The bag was offered and I took an orange cream. Never since have I reckoned 'just one' won't be missed.

Lyn Holliday

Pudding face

In the 1950s we spent our family summer holidays on the Yorkshire coast. We packed our black Ford Anglia carefully, knowing that we had to climb the long, steep hill of Sutton Bank in order to reach our destination. We were always anxious because one year the car failed to make it and we had the humiliation of having to reverse slowly down the hill to find an easier route.

We were travelling to a caravan site on top of the cliffs, near a beach where my brother and I looked forward to spending our days fishing in the deep rock pools or playing on the sands. The site consisted of ancient caravans that had not moved in years, and a clutter of converted railway carriages and old buses. As children we were delighted to be staying in a Leyland single-decker bus which still had its large steering-wheel and a push-button bell that worked. For two small boys this was bliss! We spent hours imitating the sound of an engine and running our own imaginary bus service.

The following summer we boys were disappointed to discover that Dad had booked a 'proper' caravan on the same site. It belonged to Norris Brook, one of his pals in the village. He was the local greengrocer and was well-off, fastidious and very particular as to who let his holiday home. Mum was a nurse, and a very tidy, house-proud person, so Norris had no qualms.

Mum was thrilled to be staying in a caravan. On arrival she was not disappointed; it was immaculate and decorated in country-cottage style. The small bay windows had diamond-shaped leaded panes with pretty floral curtains. It had cream paintwork and soft patterned furnishings. Mum loved the small convenient kitchen; she had brought her new pressure cooker, thinking it would be ideal in a small space. After a day at the beach we would return, hungry and tired, and Mum would make the meal while we played outside.

One evening she decided to make rice pudding, which was one of our favourites. My brother and I were playing cricket with Dad. He liked to bat and was so good at it that we rarely seemed to get him out, and had to run all over the site to retrieve the ball. A loud shriek came from the caravan and a moment later Mum was calling to us from the doorway. I can't recall her actual words, I just remember running. She looked really shocked, and was shaking with fright as she pointed inside. I was the nearest and the first to see the hissing, erupting pressure cooker spraying its contents all over the ceiling, the walls and furnishings. Dad dashed straight in and turned off the gas, yet the scalding rice pudding kept on blowing. We stood outside for what seemed a long time waiting for the pudding to subside. Mum was in tears, and the caravan was a mess.

The cleaning-up took ages. The pudding had already begun to set on the ceiling and congeal on the carpet and it was with great difficulty that we removed it from the leaded joints of the small-paned windows.

Mum lives alone now, in frail health but still batting at ninety-one. She still likes rice pudding, but these days it comes out of a tin.

Peter Carver

Heat of the moment

It was a hot summer. I cannot remember why a new teacher was taking us for some of our lessons; perhaps he was a student. Whatever the reason, he had very definite ideas. He deplored the cinema and the boys' desire to emulate James Cagney or Roy Rogers, and the way we girls drooled over the sequinned gowns of Greer Garson or Alice Faye. Such things were for adults. He also said that we wore too many clothes. We all sat up at that. He told us we should take off our outer clothes when we went out to play. This was better than learning the nine-times table. We rolled our eyes at one another in delicious anticipation.

When playtime arrived we wondered if we could do it. Dare we do it? Our primary school had only a concrete playground that flung the heat back at us, but the notion was very tempting. Soon, the boys stood bare-chested in their grey flannel shorts, and the girls flung aside their cotton frocks to reveal vests and knickers in an assortment of colours. Out we whooped like demented nymphs and satyrs.

The word went round and interested onlookers watched as we leapt and raced and performed handstands to show how liberated we were, thoroughly enjoying our fifteen minutes of fame. At the end of break, we returned to our classroom and reluctantly put on our clothes. All except Dawn.

She had long, wavy hair, and the sun had flicked a few freckles across her pert nose. She declared she was staying as she was, and sat down firmly on her locknit knickers. Our regular teacher arrived and looked very surprised when, backed up by the rest of us, she assured him she had acted on orders. He told her he would prefer it if she wore her dress. Dawn moved out from behind her desk, rolling her eyes to the ceiling. Slowly, she picked up her frock, shook it and smoothed the creases. She adjusted her vest. Our teacher said he realised why she was often late for school. She peeped at him from under her lashes, grinning. By now, she had the complete attention of the silent class. Fifty-one pairs of eyes watched her slide her arms gracefully into the sleeves of her frock, swaying a little as she did so. She had some trouble with the neck but at length her head emerged and she shot a triumphant look around the room. I glanced at the teacher, and saw from his face that he now felt it might have been better to ignore Dawn's state of undress. She pulled at the frock and wriggled her hips until it fell to her

31

knees. Her fingers fumbled at the button holes, so it took an inordinate length of time to fasten the frock at the back. But she was not yet finished.

The sash had to be twirled and straightened, then the bow had to be tied, and retied at the back. Finally, she slipped her hands behind her head and lifted her hair free of the frock, shaking and flicking it round her shoulders. She slid back behind her desk, raised her eyebrows and rested her chin on her hand. It was a magnificent performance.

In a year or two, we moved on to secondary schools and I never saw Dawn again. I wonder how many of those in that overcrowded classroom, smelling of chalk and children, remember that day.

I wonder if Dawn herself recalls it?

Susannah Clemens

Oranges are not the only fruit

For as long as I can remember, the old man used to preach
on market days. Every Sunday he would stand in the same
spot and read aloud from his battered old Bible. I don't
know if he read the same part every week or if he used to
select a certain passage for each Sunday of the year. I never
listened to what he was saying. I don't think anyone did.

When I was a very young boy I always wanted to watch
the old man. I think that the idea of a man who stood outside
every Sunday in his best suit and read to people fascinated
my young mind. But my mother always had more things to
buy and so she would drag me away from him. In my adult
years, however, when I went to the market for my own
shopping, I would allow myself to sit in a café and watch
him. He still fascinated me. He dressed in the same
immaculate way and held his Bible out in front of him. He

33

read from the book but I am sure that he knew it by heart. Nothing ever seemed to distract him.

His chosen spot was on the busiest street corner. He would be in everyone's way and there would always be people pushing and shoving, trying to get past him. There were people shouting and bargaining, the normal noise of a market on its busiest day. He would be unfazed by it all, preaching the Word to the masses.

I remember one particularly hot summer Sunday. I had walked past the old man earlier in the day while buying my groceries and noticed that he was sweating like everyone else. When I had bought all that I needed I sat at my usual table in the café and watched the old man from there. I saw a small child being pulled along by her mother in the same way that my mother used to pull me. The mother bundled past the old man without even noticing him. The little girl, however, was looking at him over her shoulder as her mother pulled her away.

Suddenly, the girl wriggled her hand free from her mother and ran back to the old man. She dodged through the crowd quickly, as only children can do, and stood next to him. She reached into a small bag she was carrying over her shoulder and pulled out a mandarin. She tugged on the leg of the old man's trousers and, for the first time since I had been watching him, he stopped reading. He looked down at her as she held up the mandarin to him as a gift. The old man took the mandarin from her and they exchanged a few words. I was too far away to hear what they said to each other.

By then the girl's mother had fought her way through the

crowd and finally caught up with her daughter. She grabbed her daughter's hand and pulled her off again into the crowd where they soon disappeared. The old man watched her go. He was smiling. He held his Bible in his left hand and his mandarin in his right. He stood for a couple of seconds and then turned and walked away. I followed him with my eyes but the crowd soon swallowed him as well.

That was the last time I saw the old man. The next Sunday came and he was not in his usual position. The same has been true for every Sunday since then. I still look for him but I know that he isn't coming back.

Christopher Hooper

Bonfire night

In September 1958, when I was seven, I went to stay with my grandparents in Bognor Regis. One evening, having been put to bed at eight o'clock, I could not sleep, and instead stared out of my bedroom window at the moonlit garden. Suddenly a bright red glow appeared in the sky, followed by a shower of golden sparks. Someone, somewhere, was having a bonfire, and it looked so alluring that I decided to go and investigate. Dressing hurriedly, I climbed out of the bedroom window into the branches of a convenient pear tree, shinned down it, tiptoed to the shed, got out my new green bicycle and pedalled off down the lane at the back of the garden in the direction of the orangey-red glow.

Soon I came to a field bounded by a thick hedge. The bonfire was obviously behind this hedge, for I could now hear its fierce crackling and see spiralling smoke and more showers of sparks. I left my bicycle on the grass, crept up and peered through the hedge. Arranged in a semicircle in the middle of the field were three traditional gypsy caravans, painted red, yellow and blue, two round white tents, three tethered piebald horses, a group of gypsies seated round their roaring log fire and several mongrel dogs prowling about. It was one of those dogs, a small white terrier, which sniffed me out and barked the alarm. At once a man got up from the fireside and came towards me. I crouched down in the long grass, but he caught sight of me in the moonlight and said in surprise, 'Well I'm blowed! It's a little kid. What are you doing here, missie?'

The gypsy was tall and thin, with jet black hair and dark, flashing eyes, but he had a kind smile, and I wasn't afraid of him. So I told the truth: that I had glimpsed the bonfire from my bedroom and come on my bike to see what it was. 'And are you hungry after your ride?' he asked, not bothering to reprimand me for being out so late on my own as other grown-ups would no doubt have done. I found that I was ravenous and moreover that a delicious, tantalisingly exotic smell was coming from a large saucepan on top of two bricks at the side of the fire. So I just replied, 'Yes.'

'Come in through the gate, then,' my new friend said, 'and we'll give you a bite to eat and see you safe home afterwards.'

The gypsies were sitting on cushions, square pieces of carpet or old sacks. A girl of my age made room for me on her sack, asked my name and all about my family, and told me among other things that the gypsies were only camping in the field for one night, and would be going on to Arundel the following day.

The girl had long, black plaits, and wore a very dirty, torn summer dress, but her smile was as engaging as that of the man who had come to the hedge, and I thought she was probably his daughter. The adult gypsies asked me very few questions, as immediately I was seated an old woman took the lid off the saucepan and ladled stew into the miscellaneous cracked and battered tin and china plates in front of her. And everyone was soon too busy enjoying the good food to be inquisitive. Exactly what was in that stew I don't know. But it was composed of chunks of unbelievably tender white meat, tasting a bit like chicken, shreds of darker meat that could have been wood pigeon, carrots, onions, mushrooms, potatoes and a variety of subtle, aromatic herbs that I had never tasted before. It was the best stew I have ever eaten.

When I had finished supper two young gypsy women walked me to my back gate and left me without a word of reproach. I returned the bicycle to its shed, climbed back up the pear tree, and was soon asleep in bed, my escapade undetected, and not to be revealed to a soul until long afterwards.

Alison Barnes

Costume drama

In the late 1950s no one we knew had a car so family outings had to be planned with reference to bus timetables and radio weather forecasts. But the latter were only reliable if you planned to visit the fishing grounds of the Faroes or the Dogger Bank, so most people took a glance at the sky and trusted to luck.

It was a fine, warm lunchtime when – by way of three Sunday-service buses – we reached the River Bollin from our house on the outskirts of Manchester. Our picnic comprised boiled-ham sandwiches, crisps (with an individual portion of salt in a twist of waxy blue paper) and, as a horrible, unrecognised portent of what was to come, fairy cakes. There was a flask of tea for Mum and Dad, and dandelion and burdock for my sister and me.

Then it was time to change into bathing costumes for

splashing around in the river. My sister, aged five, paddled in the shallows while I attempted to increase the number of crawl strokes – about a dozen – I had learnt with the cubs. Mum watched us. Dad read his paper. Other families were doing more or less the same things, while a group of unaccompanied boys were climbing up and down the overhanging banks of the river a little further downstream. When my mother decided it was time to begin preparing to leave, she called us to come and get dried off, and helped us change back into our street clothes. 'Right,' she said. 'Five minutes to run about while I pack away. Don't get dirty!'

The climb up and down those grassy riverbanks was a great temptation to a ten-year-old, and one I couldn't resist, though I soon began to wish I had: parts of the climb were tricky, and my hands and knees were becoming grubby and sore. My clothes, I realised, though by no means filthy, were no longer clean enough for Mum's exacting Sunday standards. Worse still, I knew I was going to have trouble completing the climb. Then I fell. But the river was deep enough to ensure I wasn't hurt and my dozen strokes to the bank meant I didn't drown. But my mother's answer to the problem of getting me home without me 'catching my death' was to dress me in my sister's almost dry stretch-nylon swimming-suit. The costume was pink and ruched with a bow at the back. I protested, looking to my father for male support. My father looked away and Mum was adamant. On my feet I wore my own squelching shoes. Oh, the mortification!

Waiting at three different bus stops was torment. Girls

giggled behind their hands; boys of my age and younger openly sniggered. Standing (I wasn't allowed to sit) and holding my sodden clothes as the buses took us home, I felt that sense of shame and humiliation that only a 10-year-old 'tough guy' can feel. The 200 yards from the bus terminus to the sanctuary of home is branded on my psyche. There I was in my sister's swimsuit, clutching the pathetic dripping emblems of my boyhood to my chest in an attempt to hide the fact that my mother had insisted I wore it fully done up. Each step I took sounded like a half-submerged hippopotamus breaking wind.

The word spread like wildfire. Front doors opened and banged shut as more and more smirking kids swelled the audience. The dread word 'sissy' seemed to be on every lip. By teatime every child on the estate had heard the story, and I knew that this day was one I'd never be allowed to forget.

Brian Smith

About a boy

In 1937 I was eleven years old and my sister six when our mother contracted double pneumonia. She was ambulanced to the Edinburgh Royal Infirmary and died the following day. She'd had chronic heart disease. My father took me to see her body laid out in the mortuary. I'd never seen a dead person before. My mother's eyes were closed as if in sleep. Her face was serene, showing no signs of the pain she'd suffered during her illness. I half-expected her to open her eyes and say, 'William, I'm feeling well again; let's go home.' It was at the funeral, as I watched her being lowered into a dark, cold grave, that I understood the stark finality of death. I wept then as never before or since.

Without Mother, my father, disabled from wounds inflicted during the First World War, was unable to care for me and my sister. Consequently, we were placed in the care of the Children's Shelter in Edinburgh. From there we were transferred to an orphanage in the countryside near Glasgow, a collection of detached houses within a spike-walled enclosure. The houses were divided into boys and girls. Each house was run by a man or woman who had to be addressed as 'Father' or 'Mother'.

Five days after I arrived, two boys in my house began to fight. I stepped in to separate them. Suddenly I was knocked to the floor by a blow to my face, and as I lay there bleeding from a split mouth I was hauled back to my feet and struck again. It wasn't one of the boys hitting me, it was the house father who had decided that I was the instigator of the fight. He further punished me by denying me dinner and supper that day. I asked the boys if anyone had ever tried to run away. A few had tried, they said, but had been caught and flogged by the house father. Despite this, I decided to try my luck.

After midnight, with everyone asleep, I dressed in my summer jersey, shorts, soft shoes and no socks. I shinned down a drainpipe from my dormitory window. In the bright moonlight, I kept to the shadows, and made my way to the perimeter wall. Unable to scale it, I moved on to the chained iron gates. By pulling on the slack chain, I opened the gates enough to squeeze through and out on to the public roadway. With no idea of direction, I ran blindly over fields, down winding lanes and forest tracks, startled by screeching animal noises.

About midday I reached the outskirts of Glasgow. My aim was to get to the Edinburgh Children's Shelter and report my story. I asked a gentleman which direction it was to Edinburgh, and how far to walk. He asked me where I'd come from. I said I'd been on holiday with my aunt, didn't like her and wanted to go home to my mum. I must have looked a sorry spectacle. The man took me to his home. His wife washed the blood from my bruised feet, gave me a pair of her husband's socks and a meal, and afterwards took me to Glasgow station where they bought me a ticket to Edinburgh. They waved goodbye; it was the last I saw of them.

I reported my story to the matron of the Children's Shelter. An enquiry team from the RSSPCC was sent immediately to check my allegation of flogging and bullying by the sadistic house father. The boys verified my story. The house father was dismissed. When I was returned to the orphanage, I was cheered as a hero for having liberated the boys from tyranny. The orphanage no longer exists but 'William Aitchison, absconded 1937' is still on the record books.

William Aitchison

Up the creek

In the late 1940s, when my cousins and I started spending our summers in a hut on a beach, there was no bridge over the creek. To reach the sea, people had to park by the road and walk to the rowing-boat ferry that operated across the mouth of the harbour at the other end of the beach. We soon noticed, however, that many people turned off the road and took the path past the knoll, because this seemed to head more directly towards the huts they could see ahead of them. Thus they arrived at the creek, sometimes attempted to gauge its depth, but eventually, unless the tide was very low, disconsolately retraced their steps to the road. We spotted the opportunity and every morning after breakfast we marshalled our fleet of ramshackle wooden dinghies on the far bank of the creek. There we would watch for the first heads emerging from the scrub by the

45

knoll and prepare for the sell. The conversation went along these lines:

'Would you like us to row you across the creek, sir?'

'How deep is it?'

'Oh, very deep, sir.'

'How much do you charge?'

'Whatever you like, sir.'

The pricing strategy was derived from the official ferryman. It was a good policy because, although 6d a head was the norm, half-a-crown was not unusual, and this was riches indeed.

One morning, the tide was high with a strong south-westerly wind blowing up small waves on the creek. Our only craft was a very small dinghy with one half of the transom broken off from the sculling rowlock. We were pleased not to have to wait too long before we spotted two people approaching. However, as they came nearer, their appearance made us distinctly nervous. The man was large and middle-aged, in a three-piece pinstripe suit, complete with watchchain and fob. His companion was an elegantly dressed young lady. A hurried conference established that we would have to take them over one at a time and, as the oldest, I would be the ferryman. The sales pitch went much as usual, and the man was helped aboard.

The stem thwart creaked alarmingly. I took the oars and my cousins pushed the little boat out. Halfway across, I noticed with rising panic that the freeboard at the broken transom was not much more than an inch. I asked my passenger to lean forward. The custom that, when at sea, one should obey all lawful commands without demur is a wise one. He demurred and, when told the reason for the request, leant back to look. The stern went down and the boat sank. At this point, my passenger was still dry from the waist up and should have merely stepped out. However, having been told of the creek's great depth, he cast himself upon the water and struck out with an impressive overarm. He crawled dripping on to the bank, the drops of water running prettily through the links of his watchchain and dripping off the fob. The young lady, still safe and dry on the far bank, was doubled up with laughter. The man was already trudging off towards the café.

Any pretence regarding the depth of the water was now pointless so we emptied the dinghy, sat the lady amidships and I, being wet anyway, pushed her across. After ensuring that her companion wasn't looking, she smiled charmingly, gave us a handsome tip and tripped elegantly after him.

Michael Willcox

Animal Instincts

Jobs for the boys

I was knocking on the door of the Co-op grocer's before it opened. The Boy Scout bob-a-job week was quite competitive: there weren't many 'job' opportunities in our small Yorkshire mill village for all the members of the troop, and I wanted an early start at the largest shop in the village.

I envisaged weighing out raisins in the blue sugar-paper bags, bagging up the sugar, or cutting, weighing and wrapping chunks of butter out of the large tubs that came from New Zealand. Perhaps I might be of use making up the customers' orders, helping to fill the assorted cardboard boxes that spread across the floor waiting to be collected. The manager – a rather dour man – opened the door. He wore a jacket and tie and, like all his staff, a knee-length white apron, crisp and gleaming, above polished brown shoes. I was wearing my scout uniform, so I think he knew what I was there for. 'Come in, lad. So you want a job do you? Now, let's see, things are a bit busy this morning what with the orders, but I'm sure we can find something for you. Can you come back about four o'clock this afternoon?' I was thrilled. My first promise of a job.

My next stop was Albert Garside, the joiner and undertaker, a few hundred yards up the hill from the Co-op. He immediately set me to work in his joiner's shop. On a stand in the middle of the workshop was a gleaming new oak coffin; the wood smelt lovely. He wanted me to lime the oak with a mixture of lime and beeswax and, after a quick demonstration, he left me. It was hard work and took ages – there's a lot of surface area on a coffin. But it polished up well and Albert seemed pleased with the result and gave me three times more than a bob – fifteen pence. He took the JOB DONE sticker and put it in his workshop window to deter other scouts from knocking at his door.

The money was starting to roll in. I knocked on several house doors and did a series of jobs which included cleaning windows, scrubbing and scouring a front step, mending a puncture on a bike and taking two dogs for a walk. It was quite a heady experience to be given money for one's work, and the more I laboured the heavier my pockets felt. I liked it!

Towards four o'clock I headed back to the Co-op, by which time it was getting dark and I was tired. 'Follow me, lad,' said the manager, as he led me into the back storeroom. It was large and cavernous – not as well lit as the shop, full of boxes, sacks and smells of all kinds. It seemed quite chaotic. A cat sat flicking its tail. 'Here you are, lad. Here's a job for you,' he said, giving me a sack and a large bucket of water. 'Over there are some kittens; we want them drowning. We need cats to keep the mice down but we've got too many. I'll leave you to it.' He walked back into the shop.

I hesitated but felt committed to do what the man asked. The movement of those small animals in the sack in that bucket of water unsettles me still. I told no one what I had done at the Co-op. It ruined my day and I hated that sticker in the shop window that said JOB DONE.

Peter Carl

My friends and other animals

A friend of mine lived by a creek in Nigeria. He had a collection of animals, including a monkey (which shared a cage with a very large rabbit), a donkey, a camel – and a crocodile. One afternoon he rang and invited me to tea. Sitting by the creek, watching the sun go down below the palms and mangroves, anticipating the first 'real' drink of the day, was always a pleasant way to relax, and I gladly accepted, as I had done many times before. But this time was to be different.

The usual group of friends were on the verandah helping themselves to tea and sandwiches. As I joined in, I noticed my friend walking down to the crocodile pool. He waved to me to join him, which I did, reluctantly. I had seen quite a few crocs during my travels and the novelty had long worn off. I may be an 'animal person' but crocs have never been close to my heart.

I was standing looking at the thing in its small pool when my friend asked me if I would give him a hand. I was instantly suspicious. 'To do what, exactly?' I asked. He replied that he could see the animal had outgrown the pool and he now wanted to release it into the creek. I pointed out that he was asking not just for a hand but also for an arm, and probably a leg. But, being a soft touch, I agreed – provided he took the sharp end and I took the tail. Big mistake! I really should have twigged when he agreed with great alacrity.

That he knew a good deal more about crocodiles than I did rapidly became clear, when he expertly placed a noose around those terrible jaws. The animal barely reacted and I was lulled into a false sense of security. This was dispelled when I reached down, grabbed the tail and went head over heels, much to the enjoyment of the group on the verandah (they had brought the drinks out and settled down for the entertainment).

When we had finally manhandled the struggling beast to the edge of the creek, I told my friend under no circumstances to release the jaws until I was back on the verandah with a drink in my hand. He promised, so I set off up the lawn. When I was halfway there, the people on the verandah leapt up, shrieked and fled inside. I sensed something had gone wrong. Looking over my shoulder I saw the crocodile running at an unbelievable speed straight at me without its noose. I realised that I could not make it to the verandah (which was now deserted, with the bungalow glass doors firmly shut), so I ran towards the nearby monkey house, accompanied by shouts of 'Run, run!' from my friends.

As I approached the monkey house – the crocodile rapidly gaining – the monkey, which had been closely following these events, panicked and jumped on the rabbit, both of them screaming loudly. I now had the choice of facing the croc or diving into the cage of a deranged monkey which could well try to do to me what it was doing to the rabbit. I was not too keen on either option but the problem was solved for me when the monster suddenly swerved and ran straight back into its pool. When the hysteria had died down, and I had had my first drink, I thanked the gang for their shouts of encouragement at a difficult time. They looked surprised and someone said, 'But we weren't encouraging you, we were cheering on the crocodile.'

Robert Cubin

Flood alert

'You'll never keep thae birds on running water,' grumbled my grandfather the day my granny installed a dozen Khaki Campbell ducks on the stream which ran alongside their cottage. Gran didn't reply, but she was quietly determined, and he knew better than to interfere further in matters domestic.

I was sitting at the kitchen table with Gran one early spring afternoon when we suddenly heard a low vibration like distant thunder. Gran jumped to her feet and made for the door, motioning me to follow. She picked up her long skirts and set off, not towards the roar, but in the opposite direction with me in pursuit, marvelling at the speed of her black stocking-clad legs.

Gran sprinted along the river until she came to a spot where the flow narrowed as it passed between two flat rocks. Straddling it, she waited until presently the terrified ducks appeared, tossed about in the snow-melted waters like paper boats in a gutter. She grabbed them as they passed and flung them to me on the bank, where they struggled to their feet, indignantly squawking and flapping in fright. We saved eleven out of the twelve. My grandfather laughed when he heard about it. 'The folk at the sawmill down river will be enjoying a good supper tonight,' he joked.

I loved staying at my grandparents' cottage. From my window I could see the house where Margaret and Kenny lived. Margaret was the same age as me, a head taller, dark-haired and shy. Kenny was six years younger and totally unlike his sister, with a mass of curly red hair and freckles. We were constant playmates, free to roam, but expressly forbidden access by my grandfather to the disused quarry above the house. However, it was such a delightful place for games that it drew us like a magnet.

One day after a week of rain had kept us indoors, we decided to risk a trip there. Sometime later my heart lurched as I recognised a familiar low roar from further up the valley. 'Run! Run!' I screamed. We raced for the ledge around the quarry. But Kenny's legs were shorter and slower than ours. The approach of the bore was terrifying. The water filled the quarry unbelievably fast and the flood caught him before he could reach safety. All I could think of was my grandfather's wrath when he discovered my disobedience. That thought prevented panic from overwhelming me. Pure adrenalin propelled me to the spot where Gran had rescued the ducks. Seconds later, the top of Kenny's head bobbed above the torrent and I grabbed his hair with all my strength.

For what felt like several minutes the powerful undertow threatened to tear him away. With superhuman strength I finally landed him and he lay on the bank coughing and wailing, until his breathing gradually returned to normal. When Margaret arrived, we swore Kenny to secrecy. We returned to our respective homes and, despite my anxiety, there were no repercussions.

Years later my husband and I met Kenny at a dinner dance. He came up to us and introduced me to his wife as 'The woman who saved my life.' You can imagine I felt distinctly uncomfortable to be presented as a selfless heroine when my instincts that day had been largely motivated by self-preservation. My overriding emotion at our reunion was one of suppressed hysteria however. Instead of being covered with those strong, red curls that had saved his life, Kenny's head was blatantly and irrevocably BALD!

Frances Brown

A rat's tale

'You're frit!'

'No, it's not that, Mr Briggs. It's just we're so short-staffed at the moment . . .'

'You *are*. You're frit. You're frightened of rats.' I flipped through my packed diary.

'I can maybe fit you in for an hour a week next Thursd—'

'Just don't bother. I'll sort it out myself.'

'No, I wouldn't do that, Mr Briggs. Rats can be dangerous things.'

'There you are. You're frit.'

I winced as Mr Briggs slammed down the telephone, and pictured tomorrow's headlines in the *Evening Post*: heartless sanitary inspector and man savaged by rats. I'd have to get out there, and pretty quickly too.

It took me fifteen minutes to get to the Briggs' place. I rang the bell and heard a woman's voice inside saying, 'I'll have to go. There's someone at the door . . . You'll be all right . . .' Then she appeared – evidently it was Mrs Briggs, a pretty woman, but dishevelled and obviously very distracted by whatever was going on upstairs. 'Yes? What is it?' She kept looking over her shoulders, up the stairs. 'We're very busy at the moment.'

'I'm from the Environmental Health Department. Your husband rang earlier.'

'Oh, thank goodness! Come in.'

She dragged me inside. 'He's locked himself in the bathroom and won't come out.'

'But why? What's happened?' I asked.

'It's that rat. In the loft.'

I rushed past Mrs Briggs and ran upstairs. The loft door was ajar and a stepladder teetered at the top of the stairs. I quickly inspected all three bedrooms and, discovering no immediate danger, relaxed a little. 'It's all right, Mrs Briggs. Don't worry. I'll have a word with your husband.'

I sat down on my haunches and spoke through the bathroom keyhole. 'It's OK, Mr Briggs. I'm going to go up into the loft to check that it's gone.' A deep shudder and the sound of chattering teeth came from the other side of the door. Going back to the top of the stairs, I put the stepladder upright and climbed up. Bracing myself, I slowly lifted the loft door and, as nothing came rushing out at me, nodded reassuringly to Mrs Briggs at the foot of the stairs. But, turning back to the loft opening, I saw them: two evil, beady, shining black eyes that stared straight at me from the side of the loft door. I nearly fell off the stepladder.

For what seemed like several minutes, the rat and I just stood there staring at each other. This was all very well for the rat, but my arms were getting tired holding up the loft door. So I decided to be bold. Still holding the loft door open, I took a deep breath and yelled, '*Boo!*'

The rat was totally unimpressed. I was left wondering what to do when suddenly it toppled over on to its back with its feet in the air and its eyes staring straight ahead. I took out a pen and poked it. Satisfied that it was no longer of this world, I prodded it with my index finger. It was cold and stiff and had obviously been dead for days.

I took out a plastic bag, scooped the rat into it, descended the ladder and held it up to Mrs Briggs in mock triumph. Then, walking across the landing to the bathroom, I sat down by the keyhole. 'It's all right, Mr Briggs. You can come out now. Don't be frit.'

Keith Dawkins

Bird on the line

I was waiting on platform six at East Croydon station after a tiring day helping people as a witness service volunteer at Croydon Crown Court.

It's a bleak but busy station with nothing to commend it except for its amiable staff and a multitude of trains criss-crossing the southern counties. The shadowed station is surrounded by high-rise office buildings, warehouses and yards, and nothing more. There is no grass, no trees: just an umbrella of grey sky. But there are always pigeons about, pecking in the cracks for crumbs from takeaway baguettes or rolls. The pigeons are 'station-wise': they keep out of the way of trains and passengers.

One pigeon in particular was quite still. It was resting by a painted iron pillar, motionless, with only a slight movement of its head and eye, and its black and purple feathers glistening. Passengers walked by on either side, but it took no notice. It did not attempt to move out of the way.

The bird worried me. It did not look injured, but then again it did not look like a normal cheeky, perky, pecking-type of pigeon. Many are so tame that they come right up to your feet, looking for scraps of goodies. This one did not move an inch. I went to the coffee stand and begged two plastic lids. (I needed two because of the hole set in the middle). They fitted together to make a firm base and I poured some water from my bottle into the lid and put it down by the pigeon. The bird took no interest.

I walked away and sat down, watching. The bird did not touch the water. The makeshift container began to leak and the water trickled along the cracks. It did not even drink from the cracks.

No one seemed to notice the pigeon huddled by the pillar. No one even looked. Minutes passed.

A Caterham train was announced and people began to shuffle to the edge of the platform. The bird still did not move. Along came the train, quite fast, and almost on time for once. Suddenly, as the train drew into the platform, the pigeon rose, wings flapping frantically, and flew straight into the side of the moving train, instantly falling down on the track under the wheels. It was gone. Swept away. Crushed.

I was shocked, shattered. It was so obviously an act of self-destruction. The pigeon had committed suicide. Cats crawl away to die. Perhaps other animals do, too. But this was a bird. It should have lived in a tree, not on a station. A bird should have air, not a timetable.

Stella Whitelaw

Matty come home

Every inept first-time mother should have an Auntie Joan. In the early 1980s she lived six doors down from us. To me she was a substitute mother, and twenty years later I still long for the comfort of her home-made jam and scones. She was a gifted maker of soft toys, too, a sympathetic listener and an indefatigable babysitter to my son Allen.

She had never married and the joy of her life was a rather threadbare Yorkshire terrier. Matty yapped at the rest of the world but adored Auntie Joan, slept on her bed, and the two of them seemed to communicate in a language known only to them. Auntie Joan, with Matty trotting at her heels, was a well-known figure in the town. In and out of the library, dozing at her feet in WI meetings and doing a brisk round of the local recreation grounds – where Auntie Joan went, Matty went too.

In the spring of 1983 Auntie Joan contracted flu and was confined to bed for a fortnight. I called one morning and offered to take Matty with me for a walk to the shops. Dog lead in one hand and Allen's little fist in the other we walked the half mile or so into town. Matty was clearly not happy. She whimpered and pulled on the lead and outside Barclays bank suddenly gave a mighty yank and fled up the middle of the road against the advancing traffic. I rushed after her for the length of a block and saw with anguish Matty's tiny body disappear between the wheels of car after car before I slipped and fell on the wet pavement. I'd sprained my ankle and lost sight of her.

It was only when I'd dragged myself up that I realised the enormity of what I had done. I had abandoned my precious child in the busy high street for a *dog*. Looking back, I know that in the moment of leaving Allen I had judged that even at the age of three he was sensible enough not to run into the road. Even so it was an unforgivable risk to have taken and I still feel cold when I remember it.

Limping and distraught I dragged myself back down the street. Outside the bank stood my bewildered but stoical child surrounded by a group of sympathetic and benevolent women shoppers. But I had no time for their reproachful stares or kindly enquiries. Faint with relief and gasping with the pain from my ankle I snatched Allen up and started for home. Then the full horror of what I would have to do next hit me. How was I going to explain to my ill, elderly aunt that her beloved Matty was gone, was probably dead, and that my carelessness was to blame? Hobbling home I was filled with the awareness of what this loss would mean to her. In my imagination it would be impossible that she could ever bear to speak to me again or, at her age, to recover from the blow. By the time I reached our road I still had no idea how I was going to break it to her.

Outside her gate, wet, dirty and shivering but obviously unharmed sat Matty.

May I be forgiven. I never told my aunt. And yes I do believe in the grace of God and the guardianship of angels.

Mary Swann

Featherless friend

Six times a year, rain or shine, more than 1,000 antique dealers stall out across the windswept acres of the South of England Showground at Ardingly. Millions of pounds change hands during two days, and serious antiques, as well as total junk, are there for the finding. Somewhere between these two extremes were a moth-eaten stuffed sparrowhawk and me. He had come from a house clearance. Some loss of feathers made him valueless but his look was proud and beady and his case, though barely bigger than the bird, was well made and undamaged – a snip at £50. Despite a strong breeze, I set the case on my table and waited confidently for the arrival of a taxidermist searching for a case of the right size to house an upright ferret or a montage of mice. The breeze stiffened. In earlier and better times, it would have sent my companion wheeling and swooping across the sky, but better times were far behind him and a sudden gust merely blew him to the ground. The jolt caused a major fall of feathers. Returned to the table, my friend stood up to his knees in them. One eye was now tilted downwards to stare at the damage. The other blazed in obvious indignation at my part in his embarrassment.

The gathering gale and two more crash landings added considerably to his advancing nudity and to the malevolent gleam in his single forward-looking eye. Naked almost to his shoulders, he now stood waist-deep in down, the area of exposed skin criss-crossed with the clumsy and generous yellow stitching of an incompetent but enthusiastic Victorian taxidermist.

'Take a tenner for the bald eagle, mate?' It had started to rain and my friend, like the day's trading, could only deteriorate.

'The case is worth fifty,' I ventured.

'Twenty, then?' This was not going to be a good day. 'Difficult things, stuffed birds, mate. They don't exactly fly out.' This one less than most, I thought, as I took the money.

As a buffer against the cold, I drank most of a bottle of wine and began to have strangely affectionate memories of my semi-feathered friend. As I neared the bottom of the bottle, sentiment lurched towards sentimentality. Maudlin hovered on the slightly fuzzy horizon.

I saw him again much later in the day. He was perched dangerously on top of a handcart piled high with a day's random purchases. The intervening hours had continued to be unkind to him. The sea of detached feathers now reached to his beak. His one remaining eye stared at me, at once accusing and imploring. 'Take a tenner for the bird?' I asked.

'The case is worth fifty,' I was reminded.

'I only want the bird.'

His current owner stared, unbelieving.

'Feathers 'n' all?'

'Feathers and all.'

I gave the incredulous dealer a tenner and reclaimed my near-naked friend. The empty case was returned to the handcart which trundled away while I did my best, against the wind, to confine a snowstorm of feathers to a paper bag. An accusing yellow eye told me I still had more to do. Mere repossession was not enough.

Rain had by now softened the ground, so I buried my friend in a sodden corner of the South of England Showground using the only tools available to me – a pair of Georgian silver dessert spoons. As I turned away, a few stray pieces of down lifted up and swooped away across the sky.

Martin Parker

A dog's dinner

On a beautiful spring morning some years ago my husband and I decided on the spur of the moment to take a picnic lunch to Ditchling Beacon on the South Downs. I hastily put together some sandwiches and a flask of coffee, and we set off for the Beacon. We parked in the car-park and started walking along the footpath which runs along the top of the Beacon towards the Clayton windmills. We walked only a couple of hundred yards before deciding to find somewhere to sit and enjoy our picnic. We climbed a short way down the hillside, which was fairly steep at that point, found a reasonably level place to sit and began our lunch.

It was a perfect April day. The skylarks were singing, it was warm and balmy, and the view of the Sussex Weald before us was magical. There was no sound but the birdsong, and we started to enjoy a peaceful lunch. I poured the coffee into mugs and we waited for it to cool.

Suddenly, there appeared along the footpath a group of three people with a dog. They were chattering and enjoying the day, until all at once the young and lively golden labrador with them spotted us and our picnic. He immediately came bounding down the hillside towards us and began devouring our sandwiches, knocking over the coffee in the process. His owner, a fairly well-built middle-aged lady, came running down the hill calling his name – Billy, I think it was – and trying to get hold of him. She suddenly slipped on the dry, shiny grass, fell on her bottom, legs apart, and slid towards me where I was sitting on the ground. When we connected, we both took off at a great rate down the hill, like a toboggan doing the Cresta Run. We kept going until, luckily, we careered into a small bush, which stopped us from going down to the bottom of the Beacon and finishing up in the village. We both got up, and made our way back up the hill to where the dog had finished the sandwiches and was looking around for something else to eat. She grabbed him by his collar and, after an embarrassed apology, went back to the top of the hill to where her companions were standing. They proceeded on their way, and all was peaceful and quiet once again. Apart from her apology, not a word was spoken by any of us. It had all happened so quickly.

After they had gone, my husband and I started laughing. We still laugh about it now. It was like something out of a slapstick comedy. Needless to say, after Billy had made such short work of our picnic, there was nothing left to eat, so we went home.

Jennifer Mellor

Death duty

Twenty years ago there were live nests in the rafters. The wasps had got through a gap in the slates and had evidently been regarding my roof as their own for some time. The council, for some reason, seemed unwilling to divulge the name of an exterminator, but after I had described my problem with a certain amount of cautious exaggeration, a number was given – rather grudgingly, I thought. 'You can try,' the voice added, 'but he isn't officially on our books. It's nothing to do with us, really.' I thanked them for their help, rang the telephone number I had been given and waited.

Three days later, there he was on the doorstep. 'Have you got a bucket?' asked the man. He was short and podgy with a pale, almost grub-like face and light-coloured lashless eyes. He had a London accent with an overtone I couldn't place.

'Yes, of course,' I said. 'Do you need anything else?' It

seemed improbable; he was carrying all manner of objects –
a cylinder, a heavy-looking black carrier bag and something
that looked like half a wetsuit hung over his free arm.

'Well, I'd better take a look first,' he said. I led him up
to the attic. 'Yes,' he breathed, 'I can take them. Been here
some time, have they?'

'I don't know,' I replied. 'A neighbour spotted them
going in and out and I thought I'd better have it done before
anyone got stung.'

'I'm allergic to them,' he said. 'Brings me out in a
terrible rash.'

'Why do you do this job, then?' I asked.

He shrugged. 'Used to it.'

I indicated the cylinder. 'What's in that?'

'Just cyanide,' he said. 'I'm allergic to that, too, but you
get used to anything.'

'Don't you have to be very careful?' I asked. 'Cyanide is
fatal.'

'Yes, madam,' he said. He had a rather downtrodden
voice.

'Will it take long?' I asked.

'About twenty minutes. I'll have to get into my
protective clothing and mask first, see?' He looked small and
forlorn.

I went downstairs to tinkle on the piano while I waited.
I half-thought I would hear a hiss as the gas was released and,
ridiculously of course, choking sounds and stifled cries.
Then there was a creak from the stairs and he stood in the
hall holding out the big bucket for my inspection, his button

face expressionless. I looked at the cheese-like material where the backs of small bodies protruded limply from their cells, some pale and fleshy, some already recognisable as adults.

'Well, thank you,' I said. 'How much do I owe you?'

'That'll be fifteen pounds,' he replied.

'Will a cheque do?' I asked. He nodded and followed me into the room with the piano.

'Musical, are you?' he asked.

'Not really,' I said. 'I just like playing.'

'My daughter's musical. She plays the cello,' he volunteered.

'How lovely,' I said. 'Who do I make this out to?'

'Mr L. Kagan. Don't know where she gets it from. Doesn't mean much to the wife and me. You'd think it would. We're Jewish, see?'

'Yes,' I said, scribbling his name. 'But it helps if you're brought up with it.'

'Brought up?' he asked, blankly.

'Yes. Like, what opportunities there are in your childhood.'

'Oh yes. See what you mean. Well, the wife and me, we spent our childhoods in Auschwitz.'

Elizabeth Hogg

Bolt from the blue

Chris was one of the rough kids my mum didn't want me to play with. I liked him because he knew things that I didn't. He was a shoplifter of startling finesse. We'd go to HMV and I'd think he was just browsing like me, but afterwards his rucksack would be full of records by the Clash or Devo or whoever we were listening to then. Chris had an older brother called Kevin – a genuine thug, simple and brutal. There was only one good thing about Kevin: he had a crossbow. Chris said that Kevin sometimes let him look at it, but he warned Chris that if he ever touched it, he'd be dead. But then Kevin got sent to reform school. Chris called the same night. 'I've got it,' he said, and I knew what he meant. For months we'd talked of hunting rats in the beck, a viscous brown stream that ran through tussocky fields until it lost itself in a quagmire. 'Got to be early – five at the bridge,' he said.

I slipped out into the morning, before the milk, before the dawn. The air was dense with cold. And there, at last, was the fabled crossbow: wood worn smooth, steel bright and springy, wire taut as a harp-string. The walk was half a mile and we two hunters did not speak. The thrill of death was on us: we were tense and reverent, our heads bowed. The dog nearly ruined things. It kept snuffling and whining around us – just some hollow mongrel the colour of sick. The gypsies had left it behind and there was something wrong with its leg. It was only being friendly, but we didn't want it with us. I threw a brick and it ran off.

Chris's hand came up. The place. He turned and signalled 'down', his finger pointing to the earth. We squatted like toads on the bank. And there we waited for the rats. But no rats came.

Chris held the crossbow, his thumb rubbing against the grain of the wood. I was desperate for a go, but I didn't want to push it. Finally, when it was nearly time to leave for school, Chris gave me the crossbow. I nestled its gun-like weight, its intricate mass, its coils and cogs. I knew it would only be mine for a few minutes, but that made it all the more precious. I could feel the power of it thrumming in my hands. Light came, but still no sun, no rats. 'I need a piss,' said Chris. He sent his stream across the beck, high-arched. Just then the sun rose slyly from the earth. Its light caught Chris and blackened him, and something magical happened. Through the high arc, by some prismatic twist, a rainbow appeared, shimmering in the air like a kingfisher. 'Look, look,' said Chris, his voice crackling with the joy of it. Then his face changed. 'Watch it,' he said, sharply. I was pointing the crossbow right at him. 'Sorry.' I felt a fool.

And then I saw the mongrel dog, tracking over the field towards us, eager again for companionship. 'Watch this,' I said, aiming in front of the wretch to scare it off. But I hit it in the neck. Chris snatched the spent crossbow from my hands and ran over to the dog. The bolt had gone through its windpipe. It was moving its legs. Brown eyes looked up at us, imploring. 'You'll have to finish her now,' said Chris. 'I'm off.' He turned his back. I was alone with the dog. I bent down and stroked her nose. She tried to lick my hand. I didn't know what to do. I walked away then came back. I saw a white plastic bag in the grass. I covered her face with it, and stepped down hard on her skull. Without looking at what I'd done, I ran home.

Chris and I never spoke of the dog, and we stopped being friends. He started hanging out with the other tough kids, and then stopped coming to school. I remember it all each night: the crossbow, the hunt, the rainbow, the dog pierced like St Sebastian.

Anthony McGowan

travelleres' tales

From Russia with love

The plane was taking off in twenty minutes and I was close to tears. My suitcase was still sitting in the middle of the concourse at St Petersburg airport and the potato-faced Russian official fingering my passport was unmoved.

'Your visa has expired,' he said. This was true, unfortunately. But what was also true was that when I had checked with the visa office, they had been affronted by the suggestion that a few days here or there might be an issue. 'Glasnost!' they shouted, pushing me firmly out of the door. 'No problem!'

But according to Mr Potato Head, my visa was a problem, and one that would cost $200 to solve, $100 for each day since it expired. I was nineteen, taking a year out after school, and the $25 in my pocket was all I had. My ticket was a cheap one and was unchangeable. If I was not on the plane when it left in fifteen minutes, I would have to pay for another flight, $200 for the overdue visa, and would have to find some way of getting back into town, as well as somewhere to stay.

While I was trying to make this clear, firmly and persuasively and without crying, a queue had built up. Suddenly there was a voice behind me: 'If an English chequebook's any good . . .?' Bless posh Englishmen. He was young, with a pink face and floppy hair, and had come from several places back in the queue to offer $200 to a complete stranger. Sadly, however, an English chequebook wasn't any good. It had to be cash.

Turning away, I wandered miserably around the concourse, trying to think. I had been in St Petersburg for six months, teaching English. When I had arrived in February, without a word of Russian, the city was buried beneath a grimy crust of old snow. The snow melted and I saw the gorgeousness of the white nights, when the citizens walk the streets in the dizzying half-light of a sun that never quite disappears. I fell in love. I lived off marrow fritters fried in rancid oil; boiled eggs, tea and vodka. It had all been very interesting but very tiring, and I was very ready to come home.

What on earth could I do? I had an idea: I somehow persuaded the airport officials to let me into the departure lounge. I found the man who had been so sweet before and asked him if he would help with my plan. We went from passenger to passenger, explaining the situation, asking for a small loan and an address to return the money. People were understandably cagey. We were getting nowhere. It was less than ten minutes to take-off. Time for a dramatic gesture. I stood in the middle of the floor and cleared my throat. 'Ladies and gentlemen . . .' Perfect silence followed. I cringed.

Then, from behind me, I heard a voice. 'Come on, ladies, it could be your daughter!' And then came the cash.

Dollar bills were thrust at me – almost faster than I could keep count. Not one passenger would give me an address to return the money. A quiet man in a smart suit standing by my shoulder said, 'How much more do you need?' I needed $20. He gave it to me and I shook my head at the next person holding out money. 'I've got it.' I heard the news sweep the room: 'She's got it, she's got it!' A plane's worth of people clapped.

'Don't let them leave without me!' I raced back to the desk and practically threw the money at the official. He gaped. Five minutes later I was on the plane to Heathrow.

Kate Taylor

A big splash

I was on holiday in Las Vegas. The heat was searing and the idea of a day spent at a water theme-park appealed. I made my way round the various attractions, bobbed in the Lazy Lagoon on an oversized inner tube, sped down a flume or two. Loved the adrenaline rush, the big splash. It was fun.

The sound of screaming finally drew me to the Banzai Boggan. My eyes widened at the sight of four towering, almost perpendicular slides. I stood at the end of the pool and watched as mad fool after mad fool whooshed screaming down the slides into the pool below. Every one of them had a huge grin plastered on their face as they came to a halt on their little plastic toboggans in the middle of the water. I had to have a go.

I collected my toboggan and made my way up the spiralling ramp to the platform at the top of the slides. It seemed a lot higher from up there. The slides looked like sheer drops from this angle. I was beginning to have second thoughts, but there would be a huge humiliation factor in carting my mini toboggan all the way back down the ramp. I hovered nervously at the back of the short queue and started reading the instructions. Number one: sit on your toboggan and hold on tightly. Fair enough – I wasn't planning on doing any acrobatics on the way down. I read it again just to make sure I'd got the gist of it. Number two: lean forward.

That's as far as I'd got by the time they ushered me on, waving with their hands, impatient, impatient, your turn, your turn. I shrugged. One and two had been simple enough; how complicated could the rest be?

There was no going back now. I climbed on to my toboggan on the little platform at the top of the slide. Hands pushed my back. I was away. I forced myself to keep my eyes open – didn't want to miss a thing. It was fantastic, exhilarating. It was over in a second. I think I was screaming when I hit the water.

I still seemed to be going quite fast. The people who'd come down the other slides at the same time as me came to a stop. I sped past them. I became aware of people yelling and gesticulating at the side of the pool. One voice yelled, 'Look at her go.' Another hollered, 'She's going all the way to Caesar's.' I was approaching the end of the pool and still seemed to be going very fast. It dawned on me that something wasn't quite right. The bottom of the toboggan scraped over the concrete at the end of the pool and crossed the path. I was heading for the ornamental shrubbery. There was a lot of yelling going on behind me. Just as I was about to hit the greenery I stretched my arms up and grabbed hold of the barrier bordering the path. I came to a dead stop.

A small crowd gathered round. It dissipated pretty quickly when I stood up and everyone realised I hadn't injured myself. The attendants threw me some dirty looks. The rest of the crowd shook their heads. 'Did you see that?'

Number three: sit up straight when your toboggan hits the water. Number four: put your hands in the water to slow your toboggan down. Number five: leave the pool immediately.

Well, three out of five isn't so bad.

Lorraine Thomson

the swimmer

My father and his two younger brothers were all killed in World War I, and I grew up in an understandably anti-German atmosphere. In my late teens I decided to assess Germany and its inhabitants for myself and arranged a touring holiday in the Rhineland with my good friend, Jack.

On our first evening there we dined well at the inn where we were staying overnight. At the next table were three German lads, Gerhard, Heinz (brothers) and their friend Helmut, all undergraduates at Heidelberg University. They were also touring the Rhineland, but in their father's big, old Mercedes tourer. We got on well together and they invited us to join their party. Travelling in style in a Mercedes was a big improvement on foot-slogging and Jack and I gladly accepted.

A day or so later we stopped at an attractive inn in a village where custom decreed that one's first night should be liberally celebrated with the local brew, a delicious white wine. We all happily entered into the spirit and spent a most convivial evening on the riverside terrace behind the inn. I think I must have been shooting a line about my prowess as a long distance swimmer, because Gerhard bet me twenty marks I would not swim the river.

Always a sucker for a dare, I quickly stripped to my underpants and dived in. The river was wide and fast-flowing and considerably colder than I had expected. However, I struck out for the far bank and eventually landed, very sober and a long way downstream. There was not a bridge in sight so I had no alternative but to plunge in again and swim back. When I finally made the riverbank I was still several miles downstream, and had somehow managed to lose my underpants in the swim. I had a vague idea of hitching a lift, but it was now after 1 a.m. and the few cars that passed understandably gave me a wide berth.

My best bet seemed to be to find a bit of sacking from a nearby farm to cover my nakedness, but as soon as my search began, every dog in the neighbourhood started barking. Inevitably the farmer appeared, in his nightshirt, carrying an efficient looking shotgun. There was nothing for it but to try to explain my predicament in my halting German. As I spoke, a broad grin spread across his face and by the end of my account he was roaring with laughter. He took me in and gave me a shirt and a pair of trousers (a bit short in the leg but ample around the waist). To my eternal gratitude he insisted on giving me a lift back to the inn.

I had been missing about three hours and Jack and my German friends were delighted and relieved to see me. Their pleasure was not shared by the two policemen they had summoned, and I gathered I was being threatened with the Teutonic version of wasting police time. However, the farmer put in a kind word for me and I escaped with a warning against future irresponsibility. Gerhard duly honoured our bet, in fact he gave me forty marks as I had swam both ways – riches indeed!

Several years later I made a third Rhine crossing, this time under enemy fire, but that is another story.

Ray Smith

Greek odyssey

When a taxi finally stopped in front of me I bundled myself quickly in, thanking my lucky stars I had left the rain outside. I had been waiting on a wet and windy street in central Athens for almost an hour, trying to flag one down. I had been living in Greece for six months and because I had just finished my weekly Greek lesson, I confidently explained to the driver where I wanted to go.

'No problem!' he said, catching my eye in the mirror. 'But I have an errand first. Don't worry; it won't take long.'

I wasn't worried; nothing could make me give up this taxi now that I had it.

'It's just at the next corner, so I won't start the meter yet,' he assured me.

'Fine,' I said, glad to be heading home at last. It was 6 December, the feast of St Nikolaos and a day of celebration for everyone named Nikolaos or Nikoleta.

'It's my niece's name-day today,' my driver said. I smiled.

'It's my husband's name-day, too.'

We pulled in at the next corner and my taxi driver unexpectedly produced a bouquet of flowers from the front seat.

'I bought her these,' he declared. 'The florist wanted to charge me for delivery. Five euros!' he added with a hint of outrage. 'Five euros, to drive around the corner!' The nature of his errand was becoming clear. He loosened his seat belt. 'She lives down that street there.' He pointed. I nodded. 'The big white building, just where those pine trees are.' I nodded again.

Then my taxi driver turned round to face me and held out the bouquet. 'If you could just take these down to her and say it's a delivery from the florist?'

A few shocked seconds passed until I finally said all I could think to say, which was, 'But I'm a foreigner.'

'Oh, that doesn't matter,' he said, scribbling his greeting on the back of a business card. 'I can't go because she'll keep me chatting all day and I have work to do. It's number twelve. Just say you're from the florist.'

A few minutes later, after some ineffective protesting, I found myself pressing a stranger's bell and announcing in my best Greek that I had a delivery from the florist. The door buzzed open and a pretty blonde woman hurried down the stairs, thanked me for the lovely flowers, and asked me to wait. A minute later she was back with my tip. Blushing, I insisted it wasn't necessary and hurried back down the street, wondering if this was really happening, and half expecting my taxi to have disappeared into the rain with my bag of Greek homework. But it was still there, the meter already ticking.

The journey home provided me with ample opportunity to practise conversational Greek with my driver. Who answered the door, he wanted to know. Was she young and blonde? Did she like the flowers? Did she read the card?

That evening I related my unusual taxi trip to my husband and his family. They listened intently shaking their heads, amused, bewildered and ultimately amazed that I had actually agreed to deliver flowers to a complete stranger on behalf of my taxi driver. Feeling a little silly, I tried to salvage my pride. 'Well, at least I made his niece happy!'

My Greek relatives looked at each other knowingly until finally my husband said what was by now apparent. 'I don't think she was his niece.'

Geraldine Kotsis

Johnny come lately

In the autumn of 1965 I was working in Montreal, Canada. My young colleague Will had recently arrived from England. One morning he came into my office, clearly embarrassed at having to seek my advice on a delicate personal matter. The gist of his problem was that he relied for birth control on the products of the London Rubber Company. A couple of weeks after his arrival in Canada he was nearing the end of his supply and had gone into a drug-store to restock. He was completely unprepared for the indignant reaction of the clerk, who had informed him tersely that the sale of contraceptives was illegal in the province of Quebec.

'How do people manage?' he asked me. 'No one here seems up to their eyes in kids.'

'Which drug-store did you go to?' I asked.

'Laplante's,' he replied.

'That's your first lesson in Montreal living,' I said. 'Laplante's is a French-Canadian Catholic business in a Catholic province. Artificial birth control is illegal here, but non-Catholics don't take that particular law too seriously. Try Steinberg's – they don't advertise it but they'll have something under the counter.'

The next day Will was back. His visit to Steinberg's had been only partially successful. He had approached the counter rather diffidently and asked in a quiet voice whether they sold condoms.

'CONDOMS?' the clerk bellowed, thus attracting the attention of everyone else in the store, 'I'M AFRAID THE SALE OF CONTRACEPTIVE DEVICES IS ILLEGAL IN THIS PROVINCE.'

'Right, er, fine – a packet of razor blades then,' said Will. He paid for his blades and, trying not to hurry, made it to within two steps of the exit when the clerk's voice stopped him.

'HOWEVER, SIR,' continued the clerk at the same volume, 'IF YOU WISH TO BE PROTECTED FROM DISEASE, WE DO SELL PROPHYLACTICS!'

A few weeks later, tired of running the gauntlet of drug-store comedians, Will confided that he had asked his brother, Dave, to bring a gross of Durex when he came over on holiday. 'Remember to warn him about our quaint laws,' I said.

'Don't worry, I already have,' said Will. 'Dave's a man of the world – Canadian customs holds no terrors for him.'

When the day came I gave Will a lift to Dorval airport

to collect his brother. Dave was late coming out of customs but, just as Will was starting to worry, he emerged looking flustered. 'Good journey?' asked Will as we got into the car. 'Everything go off all right?'

'Your bloody present caused me some grief at customs,' snorted Dave. 'I thought they were going to lock me up!'

It transpired that Dave had hit upon the idea of concealing the condoms in a cake tin – the fit was perfect. 'Open the bag, please,' demanded the large Québecois customs officer on Dave's arrival. 'That's a cake?' he asked, indicating the oblong parcel.

'Er, possibly,' replied Dave.

'The importation of food products into Canada is not permitted. Open it, please.'

Fingers trembling, Dave opened the box to reveal the purple and gold livery of the London Rubber Company. The customs officer took out a handful of the contents. He said in a low voice, 'The importation of these things is also strictly forbidden. Wait here, please.'

He took the box and disappeared. Fifteen minutes later he returned, accompanied by an older, grim-faced man with a large amount of scrambled egg on his uniform. The senior man placed the box on the table beside Dave's bag. 'How many of these are there?' he asked.

'Er, about one hundred and forty-four,' said Dave.

'And how long will you stay in Canada?' asked the offical.

'Two weeks,' replied Dave.

Without changing his expression, the officer picked up

the box of condoms and rammed it into Dave's bag. 'On your way, Tarzan,' he said. 'I just hope you're still alive in two weeks' time.'

Tyrell Smith

We were on holiday at a luxury hotel in Malta. We loved the place. Everything was right up our street. Then, on only our second evening, everything suddenly got even better.

We had attended a patio-by-the-pool barbecue rather than the more formal dinner in the restaurant. The food looked splendid – whole salmon, succulent steaks – and the highlight of the display was an ice carving of a leaping swordfish, a real work of art. As we went to fetch our meal from the buffet tables I complimented the Head Chef on his artistry. 'Thank you, sir,' he replied, 'I learnt the skill during my years in England.' Naturally enough I asked him where he had worked during his stay. 'The Black Rabbit at Arundel was my first employment but then I moved on to gain wider experience.'

'Oh, Arundel,' I said, 'a lovely town. You must know the Duke of Norfolk?'

He stopped serving at once. 'You know the Duke of Norfolk?' he exclaimed.

'Very well indeed – most charming,' was my innocent reply. The chef broke into voluble Maltese which, of course, I couldn't understand a word of. Every one of the serving staff, and the whole management team, stopped in their tracks.

My first instinct was to think that I had committed some ghastly faux pas, but smiles broke out everywhere and the head waiter insisted on us sitting down at our table and allowing him to serve us – this, remember, was a self-service barbecue! Somewhat confused by the sudden attention we nevertheless sat, and, doubtless to the chagrin of the other guests, received the sort of attention normally reserved for minor royalty or A-list celebrities. Just as we were tucking into our second alpine helping of salmon, a wine waiter approached with a bottle of champagne – not your run of the mill bubbly, but Dom Pérignon.

'Sir, this is with the Manager's compliments.'

At the end of our meal, as we floated gently towards the bar, the Manager introduced himself and assured us that any friend of the Duke of Norfolk was an especially honoured guest, and that he, the Manager, would take it as a compliment if we would accept this small token of the hotel's esteem with our dinner throughout our stay.

Our sense of guilt was swiftly assuaged by the thought of two weeks of hedonistic delight! But as we sat in our room later on, burbling to one another, I reluctantly decided to come clean with the maitre d' the very next day.

Next morning when I sheepishly tried to explain that my acquaintance with His Grace was limited to familiarity with the pub named in his honour, he refused to listen and said that he had had much experience of English modesty.

Given the circumstances I feel one try was enough.

John Richman

the getaway driver

After two weeks of driving around Turkey – braving the mountain road to Mugla, going as far south as Bodrum, then driving north through a surreal landscape of towering mountains and fields of black volcanic ash – we finally arrived back in Istanbul. By now our finances were seriously depleted, due in part to the rash purchase of a fabulous silk kilim. Accordingly, my husband wired his bank in London and arranged for money to be transferred to the Turkish bank in Istanbul.

Three days later we were informed that the money had arrived. It was a hot, dusty Wednesday morning. We left our hotel, climbed in the car and headed out into the Istanbul rush-hour traffic. This is not for the faint-hearted. Some bright spark was driving a herd of goats down the middle of the road, and people were dicing with death as they dodged among the speeding vehicles. Horns blasted. People shouted. It was a scene of total mayhem, enacted under a thick cloud of noxious blue exhaust fumes. Eventually, we reached the bank. Luckily we found a parking space at the side of the building.

My husband went to fetch the money, leaving the keys in the ignition and me, a non-driver, in the passenger seat. Suddenly, from out of nowhere, a tall man appeared. He confidently opened the door and climbed into the driver's seat. I shouted at him. I told him that he was in the wrong car. He grinned at me, started the engine and pulled out on to the main road. I felt beads of perspiration running down my face. As we raced along my imagination went into top gear. Was I being taken to work in a Turkish-delight factory? Maybe I was going to be taught to belly-dance for the amusement of gawping tourists? Could it be that I was being taken to a remote village, to be imprisoned and never seen again?

In a total panic now, I hit the man as hard as I could with my handbag. He continued to smile. I spoke no Turkish. He spoke no English. My screams and protestations fell on deaf ears. He skilfully dodged my blows. Eventually, the car slowed down. It stopped on a piece of waste ground, close to alleyways lined with ancient wooden houses. I knew then that I was in the oldest part of the city – a very long way from the bank and from my husband. The man turned to me, still grinning. I thought that my heart was going to stop. I noted that he was smartly dressed and sporting a bow tie. He lifted my trembling hand and kissed it. Then he left the car and disappeared into the teeming crowds. I scrambled across the driver's seat, and locked the door.

Meanwhile my husband had left the bank, only to find his car, and his non-driving wife missing. He walked for miles in the heat, finally locating me. By this time I was a gibbering wreck, and very thirsty. By trial and error we found our way back to the bank, where my husband assured me there were people who spoke English. To my acute embarrassment the man I had attacked was standing there. It transpired my kidnapper was the bank manager. We had, inadvertently, parked in his private space.

Christine Shingler

Under pressure

Saturday, 7 February 1987 began much as any other day at our bungalow on the Pacific island of Vanuatu. That is, until the chilling warning came over the local radio; a cyclone was approaching and we were in its path. We'd been in Vanuatu for almost two years, ever since my husband, Ron, took up a job there with the International Labour Organisation. We knew what we must do: tape the windows and doors against splintering glass; fill the bath and other containers with fresh water; and have candles, matches and torches handy. Then began the long wait. It seemed interminable, until the rising wind and rain confirmed our fears: we were going to feel the full fury of cyclone Uma. Soon, water was being forced through closed louvres and spreading across the floors. We were helpless against it.

By now the telephone and electricity had stopped

working, and we were developing a frightening sense of isolation. Above the roar of the 150mph wind even shouting was useless. Suddenly there came a great crash as the verandah was seized and partially ripped away. Iron railings were left swinging wildly, threatening to crash into windows and French doors. Ron was through those doors in seconds, trying in vain to control the railings. I grabbed a length of rope, with which I hoped to anchor the railings to a wooden post. But the doors were now clamped shut by the build-up of pressure and I could not reach them. Rushing to the front door on the opposite side of the bungalow I stepped out, only to be thrown to the ground by the raging torrent of wind and water. There was nothing to be done but crawl around to the verandah and haul myself up as best I could. The bucking railings defeated us and we somehow floundered back indoors where everything was now ankle-deep in water and, horror of horrors, the ceilings had begun to rise and fall in a crazy fashion. The roof was about to come off. Should we stay, perhaps to be sucked out into the mass of debris screaming through the air?

Already we had endured hours of deafening noise and apprehension. Still feeling isolated we were desperate for some human contact. We decided to try to reach our neighbours' house, if our own front door would open. It did, but an uprooted tree had jammed against it. Climbing dangerously through the branches we at last arrived next door, just in time to see their glass doors come crashing in. Water was flowing down the walls and pouring from the central light fitting. The ceilings here were wobbling horribly as well. It was just too much, and we almost resigned ourselves to our fate. But the louvred windows, miraculously still intact, gave us hope. We realised that by opening and closing the shutters we could keep the pressure inside and outside the bungalow more or less equal and stop the roof blowing off. The whole dreadful night was spent 'playing' the louvres and the roof stayed on.

In the morning, unbelievably, glorious sunshine bathed a scene of horrific destruction. The forces of nature had done their worst but, mercifully, they had allowed us to live to tell the tale.

Edwina Chamberlin

Rack and ruin

The winter of 1963 was severe, and lasted well into March. One day I was sitting with two of my best friends in our work's social club. After a few pints of ale – perhaps a few too many – we decided that we'd seek some sunshine for our annual holiday. We agreed on an adventurous drive down to Yugoslavia, but, having little money between us, we calculated the only way we could manage such a trip was if we camped our way there. Not one of us was the outdoor type – we were all camping novices – but we were not to be put off, even though the Continent was still unknown territory to most English people in those days.

July came, and after a smooth trip across the Channel we landed in Calais. Before we'd started out we'd been told that everyone spoke English abroad and that we wouldn't have any problems with the language. But that advice was completely disproved when, at French customs, a large, gruff *douanier* stuck his head through the driver's window and bawled, '*Avez-vous quelque chose à declarer?*'

Owen and Neil, sitting in the front seats, looked aghast. I could see the hairs standing up on the back of their necks. Luckily, my schoolboy French became of use. '*Deux cent cigarettes,*' I said. The customs man turned his head to the right, waving us on. As we left Calais, my friends agreed I would have to be the one to do all the talking in France.

We drove on down one of the bumpy N-roads (those were the days before motorways), and had been travelling for about an hour when suddenly there was a loud bang behind us. Owen braked hard and we looked back. Our roof-rack had become dislodged and had smashed into the road, breaking into many pieces. Fortunately, the suitcases and their contents remained intact, so we stuffed them into the rear seats, lodging me inches from the roof of the car.

We resolved to get another roof-rack as soon as we could, since we could not travel much further in that state. We soon came across a garage and pulled in. An archetypal Frenchman aged about sixty, with beret and rimless glasses, appeared from his little office. My friends pushed me forward. 'Do you speak English?' I asked.

'*Non,*' came the reply.

I decided to give it a go. '*Avez vous . . .*' I began, '. . . *un . . .* roof-rack?'

He looked at me blankly. I pointed to the roof of the car; no joy. Gesticulations and broken French continued; still nothing. This went on for some time. Meanwhile, cars were beginning to queue behind us (no self-service in those days) and the drivers were pretty impatient. Horns were tooted in a displeasing symphony; my friends and I were becoming embarrassed and edgy. I began to rant. '*Sur l'auto . . . pour l'auto . . . ici,*' I said, pointing non-stop at the roof of the car.

The little Frenchman took no notice of the angry mob of drivers behind us, the queue now spilling out on to the main road. After what seemed like ages, it suddenly dawned on him. Throwing his arms skywards he shouted triumphantly, '*Une galerie!*'

That's it, I deduced, and repeated excitedly, '*Oui! Avez-vous une galerie?*'

He slumped forwards, resting his hands on the car bonnet, and looked down to the ground. '*Non,*' he said sadly, and wandered back to his little hut.

Joseph Turner

Gentleman of the road

Autumn had been warm so far, but this evening there was a red streak in the sky over the Surrey hills, and dry leaves rattled in chill air. It would be a cold night. I was chatting on the telephone in the hall to my sister. Our conversations were usually long and absorbing, but I was being distracted. The outside door was ajar, and my husband, Alan, was talking to someone outside. I couldn't think who it could be. It was almost dark, and there was quiet murmuring going on out there. Curiosity cut my telephone conversation short, and I went to investigate. There was a strange man sitting on the garden seat against the wall of the house. I wondered why. Did he feel ill? Despite the cold, he wore only trousers and shirt and had no coat. His brown hair was thick and stuck out every which way over lean, unshaven cheeks. His age was about forty. Up to no good? A con man after our money? Thank goodness I wasn't alone in the house. Our house was well off a country lane with no near neighbours. Alan had the kettle boiling by now and was making tea.

The man spoke with a gentle voice. 'I come from Harrogate. My mother's there. She'll vouch for me. Do you know of a barn or shed that I can sleep in tonight? I can't stand hostels. I don't want to be taken to a hostel. Is there a farm building nearby?' He seemed harmless enough sitting there, talking and sipping tea: a stray; a rather childlike man. But I was still suspicious. 'Can you spare me an old blanket?' he asked Alan. Like a dog, he instinctively knew who harboured more sympathy. I reluctantly went to find one. He had said 'old', so I took him at his word and found a large, but recently washed dog blanket. I began to soften a little, and it was I who directed him to the barn in the field next to our house. 'Has it got an earth floor or a hard floor?' he asked.

'Earth,' I told him, and off he went – clutching the blanket and two pound coins that Alan had given him, but with no other belongings that I could see – to what I knew was an inhospitable, draughty building.

The barn was very near a solitary lodge where a family with four children lived. We telephoned to explain the situation. 'Well, if he's harmless,' Stevie said doubtfully.

'Well, we *think* so.' It really was growing very cold. I began to feel rather guilty that I hadn't been more generous with blankets.

Next morning he was sitting on our garden seat again, with Alan making him toast and soup. He had asked specifically for chicken soup and he discarded the spoon, electing to drink out of the bowl. Meanwhile I hunted for an old anorak. He had obviously had a peep through our living-room windows for he asked me about my paintings, and he commented on some antique tools that I had collected, which were on the window ledge.

We told him he could keep the anorak, but he said he couldn't be burdened with things. We found he had left it on the gate as he went away – journeying to who knew where.

Later on, Stevie at the lodge told me that she, too, had given him tea and toast and that after he had gone she had found a pound coin on the doorstep.

We never heard of him again, but about a month later, returning from a week away, we found on the doorstep a rusty saw and a tattered magazine about Manet. We could only think that they were thank-you gifts chosen specially to suit our tastes.

Frances Mountford

true colours

I realised I'd stumbled into a den of pilgrims during lunch at the YWCA in Calcutta. They had come from all over the world, and with one intention – to meet and work with Mother Teresa. They were incredulous when I said that I'd met her, and that she'd told me that if I wanted to help, I should go to Shishu Bhavan, the orphanage. Some of these people had been in Calcutta for months and had only glimpsed her across a crowded chapel. I'd gone to the Mother House, Mother Teresa's 'headquarters', hoping to speak to her, to see if I could help in some way. I wasn't planning to work in Calcutta for long: not a Catholic myself, I was only passing through in search of a guru. I was just lucky that she had happened to be there, and had time to meet me.

But I didn't go to Shishu Bhavan. That afternoon I

decided to go instead with two English girls to help at Kalighat, a home for the destitute and dying. Being squeamish I wasn't too keen, but they said I'd soon get used to it. I didn't do much that afternoon or the next; I probably got in the way. But by the second evening I had decided to stay for another two weeks. I'd never before come across so many unselfish people. There seemed to be an almost tangible love, and it affected me. I was nearly nice myself!

Walking up Calcutta's Park Street a couple of days later, and seeing something on the pavement opposite, the two girls with me, one Italian and one Scottish, crossed the road to investigate. We found a revolting muddle of clothes being sick at one end and excreting at the other. 'Oh. How awful,' I said. 'What shall we do?'

'Well, he's obviously dying, and Kalighat is for the dying, so we'll take him up there,' said Giannina matter-of-factly.

'I'll get a taxi,' I said, and dashed off, thankful to be useful but not too close. When I returned a crowd had gathered. The taxi driver was horrified when he saw what we intended to transport on his back seat. I'm sure he would have driven off if Giannina and Rosie hadn't jumped into the front beside him. The crowd parted to leave a space between body and taxi, and there I stood. If anyone had told me, even seconds before, that I would bend down, put my arms under where I judged the bundle's armpits to be and lift him into the taxi, I would have said, 'No way.' But I did.

We set off. The apparition was lying across the back seat with me, close to the edge, and Giannina and Rosie were happily chatting about some previous incident. After a while I stretched my arm over him and hovered my hand in the area around his heart. I was rewarded with a slight flutter. 'He's still alive.' Well, I thought, I'm really here under the auspices of Mother Teresa. So I looked at this bundle of humanity and in my head repeatedly told him I loved him.

We arrived at Kalighat where Giannina and Rosie jumped out. 'Will you ask someone to come and get him?' I shouted to their backs. The taxi driver was demanding ten rupees. That was the limit! The clock said three and I would have given him five, but to demand ten was too much. There then followed a furious row. With all thoughts of love and Mother Teresa out of the window and my true colours showing, I banged the back of the seat in rage.

Instantly, as if on a spring, the near-corpse sat up, said in perfect English, 'I'm sorry to be a nuisance,' climbed out of the taxi and walked into Kalighat.

Pauline Smithson

In the dbrink

I used to go fishing in Southern Ireland every year, staying in a town on Lough Derg, a huge lake on the Shannon. I was fortunate enough to obtain lodgings with a lovely old man called Shamus Lang and his wife. It was a perfect base for fishing: great food of the type I had heard Ireland was famous for, and no set times for meals (Mrs Lang knew that anglers kept strange hours). Shamus kept a boat on the lake and told me I could come fishing with him any time I liked. Needless to say it wasn't long before we took to stopping off at the local pub for a pint or two of Guinness on the way home.

Every year I returned to stay with Shamus and, before long, I was treated more as a member of the family than a guest – not that the Irish were much for standing on ceremony anyway. On my fourth visit I came down one morning to my usual breakfast of fresh eggs, bacon, fried tomatoes and black pudding to find Mrs Lang filling every pot, pan and vase with water. Now, one thing I had learnt about the Irish was not to ask direct questions. If something was going on and they wanted you to know, they'd tell you in their own good time. So I didn't remark on her water conservation.

When I returned for my lunch, I found the kitchen sink also filled to the brim. Again, no explanation was offered. That evening, the bath was also full. Later, as Shamus and I took the first mouthful of Guinness in the pub, my curiosity finally overcame me. Tentatively, I mentioned that Mrs Lang seemed worried about some possible water shortage. Shamus took another gulp, then sighed deeply. 'Well now, it's like this. Yer man Doyle's gone on the drink again.' And that was that.

But now I had to hear the full story. So I asked Shamus what this had to do with the hoarding of water. He paused for a moment, then it came out. Doyle was in charge of the town's water supply. Unfortunately, every few months he'd go on a bender lasting three or four days. The moment the word went round town that he was hitting the bottle, everyone would stock up with water.

I still couldn't see it. As if he was explaining to a backward child, Shamus continued. 'Ye see, Doyle may like a drop or two of the hard stuff, but, for all that, he's a very conscientious sort of feller. So, before he starts his drinking, he turns off the water supply and locks up the works, so no harm can be done.'

My un-Irish mind immediately came up with the

obvious solution. Why not have a spare key made and go in and turn the water back on? Shamus slowly lowered his glass and stared at me with as much outrage as if I'd suggested the Pope wasn't Catholic. '*What?*' he said, 'and take all the man's self-respect away from him?'

Vagn Espensen

Don't mention the car

We were all hungry — my wife, my two daughters and I — as we drove along a quiet country road about ten miles north of Schwabisch Hall in southern Germany. There were so many excellent picnic places to choose from that we were late by the time we settled on our lunch site on that midsummer Saturday afternoon. Although a little hillier, the countryside reminded us of our home in east Yorkshire. The weather was glorious, the whole world so perfect.

And then it happened: a ping and a hiss and a cloud of steam from the engine. The fan blade on our year-old car had sheared and gouged a hole in the radiator. Consternation. Then, after about ten minutes, a Mercedes containing three young men came along the road and I waved it down. The young men spoke no English and my scant knowledge of German had been acquired for the purpose of reading scientific papers. My head was full of long compound words, but I had no conversational skill. By then the steam had disappeared from the radiator and words of explanation were necessary. After watching many war films, '*kaputt*' seemed appropriate. But should my opening gambit be '*Der Kühler ist kaputt*' or '*Der Kühler kaputt ist*'? I pushed the niceties to the back of my mind and tried the former.

The young men were in a jovial mood. They got out of their car, looked sympathetically inside the engine compartment and then gave me a lift to the nearest garage, about five miles away. The garage didn't cater for my particular make of car but the young men persuaded the proprietor to telephone a different garage several miles away in a town called Crailsheim. It being a Saturday afternoon, the only person there was the owner but he promised to come immediately. With relief, I found he spoke excellent English. He collected me at the first garage, took me back to my car and disconsolate family, and connected a tow rope between his car and ours. He then drove – at some speed – back to Crailsheim. The tow rope seemed to be made of elastic, and the ride tested my driving skills to the full.

When we arrived he took us to a pleasant hotel and arranged for us to stay the night. His plan was to take the radiator from one of his new models and install it in our car by 9.30 the following morning. We considered that to be an ambitious target but at 10 a.m. we strolled to the garage and found the car in perfect working order. Because the radiators on the new models and our old one were in fact incompatible, the owner had taken it upon himself to drive in the night to Frankfurt – a 200-mile round trip – to collect a new radiator from the depot. The garage owner refused to consider payment, insisting instead that the carmaker should be responsible for the full cost of replacing the radiator. All he asked was that at some future point – and not now – we might perhaps pay a nominal amount for the tow. Meanwhile, he was much more interested in helping us plan our route for Austria and offered much good advice on how to avoid the dreaded '*Stau*' (traffic jam).

And then, before we left him, our benefactor explained that he had been a pilot in the Luftwaffe who had been shot down over England and captured a couple of years before the war ended. During years of forced labour on farms in Yorkshire, he remembered being treated with great kindness – a kindness which he was happy to repay.

John Bryant

The breast man

'So what do you want to buy?' I asked Antonella as we threaded our way through the crowds on the via Victor Emmanuel. It was a Saturday, the day the travelling market came to the picture-pretty port of Lerici on the north-west coast of Italy. Two hundred stalls lined the harbour wall selling everything from posh frocks to packets of pins. The cacophony of pop and rock, played *fortissimo* by the rival vendors of tapes and CDs, was mind-blowing.

Antonella knew what she wanted – some new cushions for the patio furniture, and a shopping basket. Graziella, her 10-year-old daughter, wanted a tartan scrunchie for her ponytail. I was just happy to browse. It was my last day in Italy and I had only a few lire left.

The cushion stall was soon located. What did I think? '*Rosso, giallo* or *verde*?' I suggested to Antonella that maybe the sunflower yellow would look good on her *terrazza*. 'Possibly, but on the other hand . . .' and without further ado she sent the psychedelic mountain of posterior padding toppling sideways as she plucked an assortment of candy colours from the bottom of the pile.

'*Quanto costo?*' Antonella's face registered mock horror as the woman named her price, and then she begged and wheedled until the poor soul was persuaded to knock off a small *sconto*.

Antonella's purse was many thousand lire lighter but she was happy, convinced that she had a bargain. I couldn't tell, having lost count of how many hundreds or thousands of noughts had changed hands.

Next to a booth festooned with elegant hand-embroidered table linen and sheets, and folksy woollen bedspreads from the Abruzzi, we stopped to admire artistically constructed pyramids of cups and saucers. '*Prezzi speciali!*' screamed a stallholder. But we shook our heads – '*No, grazie*' – and moved on, passing tables groaning with 6in-platform sandals for the fashion conscious, racks of women's dresses shamelessly displaying fake designer labels and piles of 'Gucci' handbags at nonsensical prices. '*Tutti venti mille lire* – a bargain, *signora!*'

Then we arrived at the stand specialising in ladies' undergarments. Heaps of lacy camisoles and skimpy panties in gaudy shades of pink and yellow stacked up alongside warm woolly vests and flesh-confining corsets – women of all ages and dimensions catered for.

'Why not treat yourself to one of those?' Antonella

pointed up to the rows of shoestring brassieres fluttering overhead like bunting in the sea breeze. 'Some of them are really very pretty, don't you think?'

'I do. And if I knew my size in Italian, I might be tempted,' I said. Unbeknown to me, the moustached lingerie vendor spoke English and – eager for a sale, smiling broadly – he moved quickly to my side, his eyes firmly fixed on my bosom.

'*Signora*, that is not a problem.' With the merest murmur of a '*Permesso?*', he stretched out his arms and firmly cupped the relevant part of my anatomy in his two hairy hands, lingering for a moment longer than was absolutely necessary. '*Quarantadue!*' he estimated confidently.

Aghast, I backed away. Antonella appeared unperturbed. '*Si*, forty-two will do nicely', she nodded in agreement.

Oblivious of my embarrassment, he removed the peg from a lacy little number. 'This one will fit, I think. I will make a special price. Only five thousand lire. A bargain, *d'accordo?*'

Antonella fixed him with a steely eye. 'What if it doesn't fit? Will you change it?'

'Of course, *signora*. But' – with a twinkle in his eye – 'believe me, I am never wrong.'

Jill Worth

It wasn't my idea to travel overland to Australia, but I went anyway. My friend Peter wanted to go and we had both reached a turning point in our working lives. We each bought a motor scooter, a popular and economical form of transport in 1963. Mine, a second-hand, top-of-the-range Lambretta, and his, an altogether rarer machine, a British-made streamlined Triumph Tigress, in metallic blue.

For the first few hundred miles, we enjoyed the summer, the freedom, sleeping under a canopy stretched between the bikes, on our slow southward migration.

In Austria, the Triumph began to grumble. It had always been difficult to start but now it began to cut out unpredictably. We climbed the old Brenner Pass into Italy uneventfully but then Peter's composure would be sorely tested by three or four successive breakdowns, sometimes after a mile, or maybe fifty miles. We couldn't identify why it happened but when it did, Peter would strip down the carburettor and check all the ignition system, reassemble it and it would be all right for a while.

In Milan we had the bikes serviced by Lambretta where the mechanics gave the Triumph the all-clear and drooled over its racy lines and the legendary Triumph reputation. But a few miles down the road the familiar trouble restarted and grew progressively worse. Each time Peter broke down, we would really believe that we could discover the cause. But we never did.

In Yugoslavia, the roads were unmetalled, even the North–South motorway. The Triumph became increasingly temperamental and Peter's composure reached a point of collapse. I took to riding a few miles behind. I would come across him at the roadside in the act of dismantling the carburettor for the hundredth time. On such occasions, it was best to say nothing as I had, by then, exhausted every conceivable combination of sympathetic expressions, and any comment merely met with abuse.

On a searingly hot day in southern Yugoslavia, I cruised into the main street of a small hamlet. In the middle of the road, the Triumph lay on its side like a dead mule. My friend, with feet together, was jumping up and down repeatedly on the bike, bent on destruction. He went about this, not in frenzy, but with cold, methodical intent. Up and down he sprang, smashing his heels into the panelling. It continued for minutes.

A few metres away, a peasant watched him with

unblinking curiosity and when Peter stopped, exhausted, on the road, the man walked over and put his hand on Peter's shoulder. He spoke several sentences, of which not a single word could we understand. Then he turned to the bike, gave it a huge kick on the rear tyre and turned to look at Peter for approval.

The Triumph could never be restarted. We travelled the rest of Yugoslavia with Peter and his bike towed behind my Lambretta. Over mountains, through towns and villages, until we entered Greece where we hoped to get it repaired. We knew from the service manual that there was a Triumph agent in Athens. But he had never seen a Tigress and didn't know Triumph manufactured scooters. We tried to sell the bike but learned it was illegal. If you entered Greece with a vehicle, you left with it, or you did not leave. Finally, in the Port of Athens, Peter located a tramp and negotiated a freighting charge of eighteen pounds for the scooter to be carried deck cargo to England, where it arrived a year and a half later. Peter's father collected it from Liverpool docks and the rusting wreck was waiting for him at home when, three years down the road, he returned from Australia.

John Cooper

snap happy

It was an important piece of kit, my camera. And it seemed a disaster when – while out in India documenting the surviving communities of Sidis (the descendants of African slaves, mercenaries and seafarers in India) I fumbled and dropped it on to an unforgiving floor in deepest Andhra Pradesh. Something rattled ominously when I retrieved it and efforts to advance the film or depress the shutter button were futile. My heart sank when I contemplated the implications.

The despair, however, was short-lived as I suddenly remembered where in the world I was. This was a country – one of a fast-diminishing number – that had not yet evolved to the lofty heights of a disposable culture. This was a place where things, anything in fact, could *still be fixed*.

I immediately sought out and quickly found a camera

shop, an anachronism – with its cut-glass display counters and expensive photographic equipment – in the dusty, bustling bazaar. The proprietor exuded a quiet confidence when he informed me that he was the only 'camera engineer' in town and asked me to come back the next day. The atmosphere seemed decidedly less optimistic on my return; the engineer stood waiting with the offending object and confessed that, despite his best efforts, he was unable to solve the problem. It was a 'sophisticated item' that required specialist attention. The parts and the expertise were simply not available here. Perhaps someone in Delhi. Or Bombay. A universe away, I thought.

I walked out into the already sweltering morning and stood on the pavement, again pondering my predicament, when one of those encounters took place which seem to happen with greater frequency in India. A gentleman appeared, apparently from nowhere, and offered his assistance. I explained the situation and, without hesitation or a hint of surprise, he said that someone named Babu might be able to help. 'I'll take you to him,' he said. I followed, sceptical but curious, through the noisy streets, ascended two flights of stairs and glided through an open door. A dim and dusty room greeted me, filled with appliances and machinery of every description: fans, radios, old phonographs, a refrigerator, a huge mixing contraption of some sort. Behind the counter stood an elderly and utterly unremarkable-looking man, waiting patiently as if I were expected. 'Babu,' said my guide.

Babu listened intently, nodding without a word, as I

explained what had happened. When I finished I stood still, waiting for a response from this quiet man and preparing to accept that he had not understood a word I had said. He paused, then motioned for me to give him the camera. I passed it over the counter and he took it and held it in front of him in both hands – just held it and looked at it. Then he handed it back to me and said, 'It will be all right now, sir.'

I was annoyed. 'But you haven't *done* anything,' I said.

'Just try it, sir,' my guide advised. The film advance lever yielded like butter. The shutter clicked. I gently shook the camera. The rattle had disappeared. We all smiled and I looked at Babu; his head remained stationary, his eyes fixed firmly upwards in the direction of his finger, which was pointing to the sky. 'Everyone takes things to Babu,' my guide said, 'when they can't be repaired.'

Anderson Bakewell

Sleazy money

It was late 1994. I'd been working as a nightwatchman, attempting to write a novel during the 13-hour shifts. With the money I saved, and the novel failed, I decided to head to the Caribbean to escape the London winter, harbouring some kind of deluded Graham Greene fantasy of becoming a foreign correspondent. That didn't quite work out, and the money ran out, so I had to get work. I'd landed in San Juan, Puerto Rico, and a new acquaintance knew the manager of a bar. Despite no experience, no Spanish, no work permit, no nothing, he gave me a job serving cocktails. I lived in a shack by the beach and saved tips in a shoebox in the cupboard. The bar was straight out of the Warren Zevon tune, 'Lawyers, Guns and Money'. Drug dealers rubbed shoulders with DEA agents; US émigrés with lawsuits pending lay low at the bar; and a moonlighting cop with a big silver Magnum tucked in his waistband and a crucifix round his neck was on the door.

One evening I was making my way back to the bar with some empties when I spotted a thick roll of currency on the floor, just near a customer's feet. Dennis was in frequently, unmistakable with his terrible toupee – like a Davy Crockett skunk pelt sat on top of his head – thin, neatly brushed moustache and hideous silk Scarface-style shirts. I didn't know what Dennis did, but I guessed it was something heavy. He acted the big shot, loud, brash. I figured no one dared say anything to his face about the ridiculous wig for fear they'd end up inside one of the concrete columns on the new highway out to Fajardo. 'Here Dennis,' I said, 'I think you dropped this.' He looked at the roll and his eyes lit up – he quickly pocketed it.

'Thank you, David, thank you so much!' He patted me on the shoulder. I thought nothing of it, and headed home a little later, after receiving a very generous tip, from Dennis, of course. When I came in next morning the manager, Juan, told me I'd missed some turmoil late last night. A local hood, Frederico, had lost a roll of 2,100 dollars, pulled out a gun and was waving it around, threatening to ventilate the ceiling unless the money was found. Customers made a hasty exit and the staff had had to placate him, but he was furious at what had happened.

I decided I'd better come clean, but Juan said it would be best all round if I kept it to myself. I agreed. 'I don't want to mess with Dennis either,' I said. 'He's some sort of gangster, isn't he?'

'Gangster? The guy's a beeper salesman,' Juan replied.

'He drives a crappy Nissan, for God's sake. Trust me on this one.'

Dennis was in a lot after that, buying drinks and tipping heavily, having a gay old time, while Frederico sat in the corner nursing a scotch, peering at the floor as if that roll might show up. Dennis couldn't do enough for me, wanting me to sit with him and have a drink and a cigar and watch the boxing, giving me lifts home in his battered car, and thanking me, always thanking me. I felt rotten; I'd given the money to the wrong man, and worse still to Dennis, who struck me as vulgar and sleazy. The least he could have done was buy a new wig with the money, but instead he was blowing it all on booze and women.

One night he drove past me on the main drag, bundled me into the car with the two floozies he had that night, and insisted we 'go party' in Old San Juan. I sucked down the drinks, but without much enthusiasm. The worst thing was, I kept thinking I should have kept the money myself. I could have quit the bar and lain on the beach slathered in Hawaiian Tropic all day.

Soon Dennis's generous streak dried up. The women didn't hang around him so much, and he was suddenly cautious with his tips. The free ride was over for him, and so were mine in the Nissan home at night.

David Hayles

Tickets please

On day one I was escorted to the Stationmaster's house by his son, and invited to discuss ticket options over several cups of tea and a plateful of samosas. Nothing seemed easier. The sun sank lazily in the Indian sky as I returned that afternoon, smug and satisfied with my experience. Then I remembered that I hadn't actually bought a ticket. In fact, there hadn't really been any talk about trains – and the piping hot samosas had caused me to overlook the absence of the Stationmaster himself.

On day two I again made my way to the station. As flies circled me, I tried to go about proceedings in a more orthodox manner. Warily, I ventured down the platform in search of the Stationmaster. I spotted him almost immediately; a very large man with greased-back hair and samosa stains down his not-so-freshly ironed shirt. Sitting in a chair, he invited me to join him for some tea and samosas and proceeded to talk about trains – though not the ones I wanted to catch. He assured me that my tickets would be organised 'immediately'.

Day three was still in its infancy when I found myself sipping tea and making my way through a fourth freshly made samosa. I can only assume that it was my inability to finish this that sparked the Stationmaster into action. Seemingly offended, he leapt up and frogmarched me to the station. Interrupting the staff tea break, and after lengthy discussions on the suitability of various trains, he instructed three clerks to assist me. Great dust-covered books were pulled from shelves, moth-eaten forms were filled out, and soon much of the local community surrounded us, no doubt eager to watch such rare events unfold. I was eventually informed that a ticket had been selected and – immersed in a false wave of confidence – I gladly handed over my bundle of rupees. Of course, confirmations would have to be made at the main station (a clerk would be sent 'immediately'), and I'd have to wait until day four to collect my prize.

Day four came, and I decided to send a 'courier' to pick up my ticket. My error of judgement became all too obvious a few hours later when he returned empty-handed, seemingly oblivious to the task at hand. So, reluctantly, I returned. I'm not sure what I expected – certainly the usual array of samosas and sickly sweets, but a train ticket? There was, and perhaps this shouldn't have surprised me, no ticket. The Friday and Saturday trains were out of the question – there was no way they could be confirmed at such short notice. Sunday, however . . . well, Sunday was looking promising. I was told not to get my hopes up (I assured them I wouldn't), but maybe, just maybe . . . Again I left empty-handed.

Day five, and I was greeted by a triumphant-looking Stationmaster's son, who, holding my tickets aloft like a trophy, strolled purposefully towards me, and then proudly handed them over as if they were a generous donation. Ecstatic, amazed, my joy diminished on closer inspection when it became clear that it wasn't actually the train I had requested. It did not go from the place from which I wanted to depart, nor go to the place to which I wished to journey. However, it was a train ticket, and when the Stationmaster's son, slightly taken aback, helpfully suggested that he could try to get it changed, I stole it back as if it was a treasure I could not do without.

Tim Cartwright

the kindness of strangers

Spring 1959, Tuscany: I'm seventeen years old, a student, and I am trying to hitch-hike from Pisa to Siena. It's been pouring with rain all day, most of which I've spent waiting in the hills by a bridge over a stream listening to the hiss of the rain in the rushes, and the baritone bullfrogs. The very few cars that pass by do not pick me up, and who can blame them? It is more Capel Curig than the Chiantishire it was to become. By nightfall I've reached the outskirts of the town of Empoli and it is still raining. No traffic, darkness at the edge of town. Finally, a police car approaches from the town. It slows, passes me, then reverses. Two constables in the front and, in the back, a dashing *capitano*: dark moustache, gleaming eyes, tie undone, braided cap worn on the back of the head, uniform coat draped over the shoulders. He finds out mostly by sign language who I am, where I have come from, where I am going. Then he opens the door, inviting me to get in; as I do so water squelches out of my shoes. The driver U-turns and we roll into Empoli.

As we enter the lit zone of the town the rain stops and lots of people instantly appear on the paved streets, as if in a film. The car pulls up outside a comfortable-looking hotel in the piazza. The captain leads me up the steps into the lobby and then, after a salute from the desk clerk, into a busy white-tableclothed dining-room enticingly perfumed with wine, garlic, tomatoes. We sit down at a table. The manager appears and greets the captain. I am ceremonially introduced. The captain studies the menu carefully, orders soup and pasta and veal, then turns his chair round, leans back and lights up a black cigar. Bean soup *alla toscana* arrives, steaming. I turn out my empty pockets in an attempt to convey the fact that I cannot afford the meal but the languid captain waves this away as if directing traffic to turn right. Then he contentedly smokes and questions me about 'England things': football, Bookingham *palazzo* and *la regina*. The passing Empolitani pay their respects to him as I eat one delicious course after another, assisted by a nameless flagon of red wine. Afterwards the manager shows me upstairs to a room with a double bed, crisp sheets – bliss. The captain nevertheless inspects the room suspiciously, nods his approval, shakes my hand and bids me goodnight. A hot shower, then I crawl into bed and sleep ten luxurious hours.

Next morning I am awakened with coffee, fresh rolls and jam. I feel like creeping out of the hotel but in the lobby the manager waits to wish me a good journey – not a penny has changed hands. It is a beautiful sunny morning, the sky decorated with big white clouds. Outside, at the foot of the hotel steps, a police car waits. The young constable at the wheel tells me that the *capitano* has sent him to drive me out to the Siena road which is better for *autostop*.

According to the Blue Guide, Empoli is a town of 'scant architectural interest', but it is one which I remember with glowing affection, although I have never returned there. I've often wondered why I was so lucky in the kindness of strangers: a friend who knows Italy well told me I was treated this way because religious Italians believe that the manner of Christ's Second Coming may be unexpected and it's just as well to take out insurance. I'd like to think this is still the case.

David John Walsh

Brief encounters

'I'm on the train.' Behind me a voice interrupts my thoughts. It is blokeish and too loud. A man is asking his wife to pick him up from the station – or rather, instructing her. In a bored tone he responds to questions about his trip, then rings off.

I groan inwardly as I hear him make another call. Some people, I think, can't be alone with their thoughts even on a train journey, but have to embark on some inane conversation. But this is a different kind of call – one that makes you prick up your ears. It is urgent, breathy. 'What a night,' he says. 'I'll send you an e-mail. It'll be a bit naughty.' He sounds absurdly coy. 'I'll dream of you.'

It's impossible not to guess the significance of this conversation. A man across the table catches my eye and flashes me a knowing grimace, not so much amused as pained. He stares at the darkening landscape, and I can see his face reflected, thoughtful.

As the countryside gives way to scattered suburban estates, the train's occupants are temporarily on hold. Somewhere a woman is exchanging slippers for shoes, applying lipstick, bundling children into a cold car to collect this feckless oaf. My feminist hackles rise.

As the train crawls into Woking, I can hear our Don Juan breathing heavily as he clambers out of his seat. He looks exactly as I imagined – like a former soldier gone to seed, bloated, but still possessing the latent strength and arrogance of a man who imagines himself more powerful than his life allows. The train, we hear, is to be delayed for twenty minutes, so I will have time to watch the reunion unfold.

The wife is here, as she would be. A small, 10-year-old crew-cut version of the man scuffs distractedly by her side, eyeing his father with something less than joy. She is makeover material, I think cruelly: snow-washed jeans a size too small, shapeless track-suit top, a dry thatch of highlighted hair. She has a doughy jawline, and her eyes are sunken with fatigue; but her face is illuminated by a smile as she spots her husband, and she reaches up for a kiss. He ignores her upturned face, and hands her his hold-all.

I huff inwardly and turn to look at the man opposite me, but his seat is empty. I see through the window that the husband has wandered off, presumably to find the gents, leaving his family to guard his hold-all on the platform. I wish that I could change this sad little scene – empower the woman, shame the man, save the boy from the fallout. But who am I to intervene?

An announcer blares out that the train is about to depart. It starts to pulls away but then judders to a halt. To a general tutting and rolling of eyes, a passenger leaps back into the carriage; it is the man who was sitting opposite me who makes his way back to his seat, clearly out of breath. He looks like someone who has delivered a message and is glad to be free of the burden.

I look back at the platform. The woman is watching the departing train with great intensity. Not the train, I realise, but this carriage and, specifically, the man opposite me. Her eyes have the lifeless look of someone who has just received grave news. The slack-jawed boy drags his eyes from the stranger on the train to his mother's frozen face. Slowly, the woman swivels to watch her husband as he lumbers back along the platform. As I watch her back recede into the distance, I imagine – hope – that her eyes are narrowing to a cool, reappraising gaze.

Fiona Salter

Parenthood

Lost and found

In 1938 I had just turned seventeen and was still living at home as a college student. I was waiting to move on, but fears of war and international call-up were threatening. Joy, my girlfriend with the dancing blue eyes, was the be-all of my existence, but when she said that she was pregnant the sky fell in.

Both sets of parents met and they went ballistic. Arrangements were made, but we were not consulted or allowed to meet. That was how things were done in those days.

Some four weeks later I was told that Joy had been sent to Australia to live with an aunt ('evacuated', they said). I was told it had been decided I would volunteer to enter the Navy and that I would postpone my university course until the war was over. My father was a First World War veteran, having served as a Royal Naval Air Service pilot, and it was fixed that I would attend an officer selection board at the Admiralty in London. Shortly afterwards, having been asked some fairly stupid questions to which I gave appropriate answers, a letter came – no doubt mainly on the strength of my father's service – saying that I was accepted for training and should report to Portsmouth.

Father had flown some incredible aircraft – mostly seeming to be made of cloth and wire, and bearing names such as Sopwith Camel and Bristol. I soon found myself in a parallel situation, flying things called Lysander, Swordfish and (my favourite) Walrus which, in a fair gale, literally hovered.

Soon after my release from service, my father died and I had to sort out his affairs. Among his papers was an envelope bearing a wartime postmark and an Australian stamp. It was still sealed, and it was addressed to me. It had been deliberately kept from me. The letter inside was gut-twisting – an unhappy mixture of love, distress, hope and bewilderment. Joy had a job as a drudge in a boarding home in return for food and a room with her baby.

Years later I was in the Whistler restaurant at the Tate Gallery when a dark-haired woman in her early thirties came in. I had a weird feeling that I knew the face. She walked over with a cup of tea and a scone, and simply said, 'Hello. Can I sit here?' We talked. She had an Australian accent and said her name was Jonie, after her father, who was killed in the war. She was studying art history and lived in Perth. Her mother was English. She had some photographs and showed them to me: her mother, and her father – a slim, dark lad of about seventeen. I mumbled some polite words, wished her well, said I had to go, and we parted. We never met again, and sometimes I still cry.

John Atkins

On the road

Agrippa is a plumber in the employ of Mutare Signs (Private) Ltd, a company which does just about everything in and around Mutare, a small town on the eastern border of Zimbabwe. Agrippa was at my home one afternoon replacing a wooden door frame which had been eaten by white ants – plumbers are an adaptable breed in Zimbabwe. While there, he received a telephone call which left him much disturbed.

He reported that his wife was in labour and needed to get to the hospital some distance from their home. He had called his employer but there was no transport available to assist. I felt obliged to come to the troubled man's aid. We set out in my Mazda 323 hatchback and headed for Agrippa's home not far out of town.

On arrival, we were met on the outskirts of the

settlement by Agrippa's suffering wife and two generously proportioned village matriarchs, both of whom, thankfully, appeared to be very much in charge of the situation. With their help Agrippa's wife was manoeuvred into the back of the vehicle (the boot, you understand) and the two matriarchs joined her, back seat folded down. The party set off for the hospital. Agrippa and I sat in the front vainly trying to ignore the muffled sounds of distress from the rear. The matriarchs discreetly erected a curtain of sorts between the front and back of the vehicle.

As we neared town, I stopped the car in response to an urgent request from the matriarchs. Agrippa and I alighted, Agrippa much agitated and I, if anything, more so, in terror that I might be called upon to assist in the proceedings in the back of the car. Agrippa paced anxiously back and forth; he stopped abruptly when the unmistakable wails of a newborn infant were heard to come from the vehicle. The worried frown was displaced by a broad smile of pride in his first moments of fatherhood. We shook hands vigorously there on the dusty edge of the road.

In due course the matriarchs announced that we might now proceed. I got back into the vehicle intending to continue the journey to the hospital. 'Oh no,' said Agrippa. 'Now we must go home.' Somewhat surprised, I turned the vehicle to go back. His home being on a quarry site, the uneven terrain was not accessible to a mere Mazda 323. I drove as close as I could to Agrippa's modest home but there remained some distance to cover. The new mother was unable to walk the distance. Undaunted, Agrippa set off on his own and soon reappeared in charge of an aged and much battered wheelbarrow. Gently, he loaded the young mother and the wailing infant into the same and set off for home in triumph, waving me a cheerful farewell as he went, solemnly accompanied by the matriarchs. These proceedings attracted no more than mild interest from other inhabitants of the settlement.

In some trepidation I inspected the state of my vehicle. There was no physical evidence of the drama recently played out therein. The matriarchs certainly knew their work and had managed the momentous event with the utmost discretion, so as to maintain the dignity and privacy of the infant's mother and to leave no trace of it in the vehicle. Agrippa proudly told me later that the child was named Chikomborero Mazda; the first name translates as 'Blessing'.

Vikki Winter

trial and error

In the 1980s I worked in the Crown Court as a shorthand writer, recording the proceedings and transcribing relevant parts if a case went to appeal. One trial especially sticks in my memory. My mother, who had been ill for some time, was staying with me while she recovered from yet another operation. When she was feeling a little better I asked her whether she would like to spend a day in court with me. As she was still very frail, I dropped her at the court building, and an usher with whom I was friendly took care of her while I parked the car. When I came into court I saw she was sitting on a bench in front of the dock as the room was too small for a public gallery. The court clerk informed me that it was a case of attempted shoplifting, so I hoped the trial would be over within the day and she could see the proceedings from beginning to end.

The jury was sworn in, the defendant pleaded not guilty and counsel for the prosecution opened its case. The defendant was an unkempt, sickly looking young man. He was accused of throwing a brick through a West End shop window and of trying to snatch an expensive leather coat from the display. The witnesses were called to give evidence for the prosecution: first, the shop assistant who heard the window smash and saw him run out; next, the passer-by who thought she saw the defendant reach through the broken pane, and who helped apprehend him; and the police constable who was called to the scene and took the statements. Defence counsel then outlined the case for the defendant, which was that it had been a matter of mistaken identity. The young man was called to the witness stand and gave evidence on his own behalf. In the front of the court he cut an even sadder figure and was shaking with nerves. My mother watched him with huge sympathy. Often, as a child, I had found her compassion for others hard to cope with. Children less fortunate would be brought home to share our meals, and once I was asked to give half my precious Easter egg to a boy who didn't have one.

The evidence was concluded, and the jury left to have lunch. We went to a small snack bar nearby. I began to feel I'd made a mistake bringing my mother with me. She looked even more tired and frail after the morning in court and I wondered how she would cope with another couple of hours sitting on a hard bench. But she assured me she'd become quite involved in the case.

The judge's summing-up to the jury didn't take long and the jury was sent out to consider its verdict. My friend the usher took my mother into her rest room for a cup of tea, and I joined them, expecting a long wait. But after only ten minutes we were called back into court and the jury gave its verdict: 'Not guilty.'

Afterwards the members of the jury left by the public entrance, and I was walking out with them to fetch our coats when I heard one woman say to another: 'I know we've done the right thing. Whatever he did, his poor old mum still cares about him and came to court to be with him, even when she was obviously so ill.' Chatting in the car on the way home, my mother said how pleased she was about the verdict, but she was a little taken aback when I told her what I'd overheard. Later I teased her about it and suggested that I should hire her out to sit in court as 'the Defendant's Mum' in order to gain sympathy.

Carole Boden

If the shoe fits

My husband and I were shopping for shoes in Marks & Spencer. Shopping with my husband was always an ordeal, particularly when it came to shoes; he would state his intention of buying black lace-ups in a size seven but would end up trying on several pairs of brown slip-ons in size eight. Feeling that he was best left to get on with it by himself, I sat down on a chair and watched him wander further and further away from the black lace-ups into trainer and slipper territory.

A young man came into the store with a little girl on his shoulders. Very carefully, he lifted the girl off and placed her on one of the chairs opposite me. He looked very young, about 22 or 23, and the girl was no older than three. He had a swarthy complexion, two or three days' beard growth on his chin and long, dark, unkempt hair. He wore a greying white T-shirt which had holes around its hem and a pair of paint-stained denim jeans. The girl had short, dark curly hair and big brown eyes. She wore a little cotton dress and when she wiggled back on the chair you could see a pair of once-white pants. Her grubby little legs stuck out straight in front of her and on her feet she had a pair of black school-regulation PE shoes but no socks. Her father – I assumed he was her father – had a pair of paint-splattered army boots on his.

Very slowly and deliberately the young man unlaced each of his boots and placed them carefully under his chair. I saw a shop assistant look at him suspiciously as she went past the shelves carrying armfuls of refills but the young man did not notice her; nor did he look at me or any of the other customers walking around the displays. He calmly selected a pair of shiny brown leather brogues and proceeded to put them on and lace them up. Like the little girl, he had no socks on. He then stood up, lifted her on to his shoulders and walked out of the shop. At no time had he or his daughter spoken a word. The assistant came back through the area and panicked when she saw the empty chair. She reached beneath it, pulled out the army boots and stood there, bewildered and confused. She looked at me but I didn't proffer an explanation; she didn't ask for one. She ran to the shop entrance and looked up and down the concourse but obviously could not see the young man. I watched as she agitatedly explained to a security guard what had happened and I found myself praying that the young man had managed to get away.

I couldn't understand why he had specifically chosen the

brown brogues. They seemed so unsuitable for his purpose. Surely a strong pair of boots would have been better, or even trainers. And why leave his own boots behind? He hadn't even spent time ensuring that the shoes fitted properly and I worried that he would get blisters from wearing no socks. A good citizen would perhaps have acted differently and done something to stop him, but I'm glad I didn't. I will always be haunted by the picture of that desperate young man and his silent, grubby daughter.

Terry Loader

the glass menagerie

My husband was never going to use it again. I decided to dismantle it and give it away. At 20ft x 12ft, the greenhouse was dominating the garden, the glass had gone green, and I was using the interior to store unwanted items among the tangle of entwining weeds and unused pots. The garden looked a disgrace. David was obviously not going to recover his speech or movement eighteen months after his massive stroke. I was constantly reminded of his avid gardening days every time I looked out the window. He had provided us with food grown in his beloved greenhouse for thirty years – peppers, courgettes, marrows, tomatoes, lettuce, strawberries, asparagus . . .

I remembered our moving into the house with our young children, David's laborious assembling of the greenhouse, his calling me over to hold bits upright as our hands froze to the metal. I recalled David handing our little daughter his first marrow to carry to me and how, by the time I received it, she had made eyes and a mouth for it and wrapped it in a shawl, refusing to let me cook it.

But a demanding job made it simply impossible for me to tend the vegetable garden myself. I decided to make a lawn and flower beds, and have something colourful to look out on.

It was very hard work indeed taking the greenhouse down. Every pane of glass that David had so carefully put in place had to be removed, and the aluminium frame had to be unscrewed, bolt by carefully screwed-in bolt. It was, however, the foundation that amazed me. I dug up countless bricks, paving slabs and breeze blocks laid a foot deep to make the base level and to support a low brick wall on which the greenhouse rested. I dug and dug and dug, gave away the small mountain of bricks and blocks, and levelled the earth for my lawn and flower beds. It was heartbreaking to witness David's meticulous and perfectionist work, and I felt like a traitor for undoing it all. I felt as if I were burying him alive. When I'd done it, I wished I hadn't. But when all the work was finished and I'd had the turf laid, and the red and yellow flowers were flourishing, the garden cheered me up.

After a few weeks I noticed something growing through the turf where the greenhouse had been. This was the earth where every inch had been dug down, where sand had been laid beneath the lawn, where a mound of bricks and breeze blocks had lain for several weeks before collection. They were David's tomato plants – twelve of them, sturdy and strong, bursting upwards. Strawberry plants were appearing too, and wisps of asparagus.

Of course I tended and fed the tomatoes and gave them stakes to support them as they grew fast. I transplanted the strawberries and asparagus into my flower-bed.

'Here you are, David,' I said as I gave him the first ripe tomato many weeks later. 'These are the tomatoes that you grew two years ago. Next summer we shall have your strawberries.'

David is still growing our food.

Susanne Carr

In deep water

The sun beat down on the deck as the boat chugged steadily out to sea, but the breeze and flying spray kept us cool. Dolphins rose just in front of the bows, diving down and spiralling upwards in graceful formation, always keeping just ahead. Over the fresh sea smell I caught a faint whiff of diesel and hot paintwork. It was about an hour and a half from Belize when the island came in sight, lying quite low on the horizon, with just a few shacks and some trees to give shade. As we got nearer we could see it was fringed with a white sandy beach.

The boat stopped some way off. Although the water shelved deeply, the boatman was unwilling to go too far in. There was no jetty so the boat swung on its anchor. The throbbing engine stopped, and suddenly it was peaceful, just the quiet slap of waves against the hull.

We swam ashore. I pushed my baby daughter in front of

me in her red rubber ring. It was further than I thought, about as far as I can comfortably swim, but I enjoyed the effort, the water was so clean and green. The sand felt like sugar between my toes as I waded ashore. I adjusted my baby's sun bonnet more securely, pushing my own firmly down on my head as I felt the hot sun beginning to dry my streaming body, salt crystallising on my skin.

'Took a risk, didn't you?' an American-accented voice addressed me. I wondered what he meant. There were several of us, it had seemed to be safe enough to swim ashore in a group, no real tides in that area, and anyway, we had a boat to come and help us if needed.

The owner of the voice came down the beach and offered cold beers before he invited us into the largest of the shacks.

Inside was a surprise. Laid out in an orderly fashion on wooden shelves were row upon row of bleached sharks' jaws, some large, some small, each one with several rows of those famous inward facing, serrated teeth. The wind rustled through the palm matting walls and I shivered.

'Whatever do you do with them?' we asked, looking around at the macabre collection in fascinated amazement.

'Tourist trade,' replied the sun-darkened owner laconically. 'I send them all over to Belize, and they get snapped up.' He paused: 'If you'll pardon the pun.'

I knew people did collect sharks' jaws, in fact I remembered now that someone I knew had one sitting half way up a dark staircase in Southampton. You sometimes come across one in a dusty corner of an antique shop, a souvenir brought home by some long forgotten mariner.

'Where are they caught?' I asked, although I suddenly knew the answer.

'All around here. We put down bait and all of a sudden there are hundreds of them milling around out there, just waiting to be trapped and brought in.'

He showed us how the flesh was removed, and the horrific jaws left out in the hot sun to bleach.

I looked out at the shining sunlit sea all around us, with the boat bobbing at anchor. I could make out the boatman moving around, tidying up something on the deck.

We all accepted a ride back in the outboard dinghy.

Christabel Milner

keeping mum

If you had met my father hovering in the Stanley Gibbons shop on the Strand, or battling up the hill to my house laden down with orange plastic bags stretched taut over the newly acquired first-day cover albums, you would have thought him just another almost-integrated Asian stamp-collector. His oversized car-coat was never quite right for the occasion and his thick-soled Bata shoes were the sort young boys were forced into by their mothers for the first day of junior school. He would arrive at my door, bags at his feet, propped up against the wall with one hand, inhaler in the other, barely able to speak, his airways constricted by the asthma attack brought on by exposure to the cool, damp English air, and the effort of his victory over the incline of my road. 'You should have phoned me from the station, Dad.'

'What for, when I can walk?' He did not know how to

accept with grace – not a lift, not a gift, not a gesture. As children we treated him with varying degrees of caution, and as adults we found our own ways of communicating with him.

For my part, I learnt to gain his unreserved affection through academic success. From my earliest memories of him teaching me to count, and later to multiply, using burnt-out matchsticks which I stored in a wooden matchbox till the day I graduated, I felt his pride and approval. Maybe it was the old story of the first-generation immigrant seeking success for his offspring in the revered English educational system, or maybe it was just the way we found to take pleasure from each other. But it was where we met and understood each other, until I found another place to meet him.

My third child was due in four days, and my parents had arrived in the morning to see my elder son, aged five, perform in a school play. It became evident during the performance that the contractions which I had been experiencing but ignoring for several hours were real, but, since they did not progress quickly and the play was almost over, I continued to ignore them. By the time we returned home I was in some pain and my father had noticed. 'Are you in labour? Do you know how dangerous this is, you silly girl? Call your husband and get to the hospital right now.'

I did as he said, accepting that a full-blown labour after two Caesarean sections was not recommended. But before I left I spoke to my son. 'Mummy's got to go to the hospital to have the baby. I won't be away too long, so be a good boy and look after your brother while I'm away.'

I turned to see my father sitting on the steps, his head in his hands. He couldn't explain why he was upset and I was ushered away to the hospital. I came home five days later with a new baby and my father wept. 'I remembered,' he said. 'After sixty years, I remembered. How my mother left me with my brother and used the same words as you used when you spoke to Joseph. But she never came back. The servant said, "Your mother is dead," and I didn't understand. He took me into a room and said, "This is your mother's body. After today you will never see her again. That's what it means to be dead." But you came home to your sons. I am so happy for them.'

Sara Selvarajah

Honour among thieves

When we lived in New York City, I often took my children to a small playground in Central Park. It was never very crowded because it had only a few swings, a slide and an old-fashioned climbing-frame. There was nothing to attract older children. One Friday, as I sat with another young mother, we were approached by two boys. They were about ten or eleven and had been making the rounds. They admired my spaniel and asked if they could pat her. I remember feeling suspicious because of the way they danced around us. At the same time, I was charmed. They were very funny. Suddenly, I felt my handbag being pulled from my side. One boy was already at the entrance to the playground and the other was racing towards him with my bag in his hands. I rose. 'Look after my children,' I cried.

Up, up; heading west. My heart was pounding. It

seemed that I was never going to outrun them. We arrived at the highway which dissects Central Park. Unfortunately for the boys, the lights had just changed. As they stopped, so did a police car. Two policemen jumped out and grabbed the bag-snatcher. The other boy ran on.

'This your bag, lady?'

I could barely whisper, 'Yes.'

He said, 'Take your time, lady. I need to know if you want to charge him.'

I heard myself say, 'Please, may I talk to him?' The boy was truculent. The sweet smile was gone and in its place was a sneer. I asked him, 'Why?' He whined that he hadn't enough money to buy a Big Mac for lunch. That made me furious. 'A Big Mac,' I said scornfully, 'And risk a record? You must be crazy.' Then, 'What would your mother think?'

He looked startled and I persevered. I went on and on and on. I pounded him with images of what it meant to be a mother. I spoke of pride and despair. The policeman didn't say a word. The sneer which was the boy's initial defence slid away and he began to cry. I continued. He wept. At some point I said, 'I'll let you go if you promise me that you will go home, right now, and tell your mother.' He nodded assent. I said, 'Promise me, I want to hear your promise.' He promised.

My husband was furious when he heard what had happened. He thought me naive and prophesied that the boy, far from being put off stealing, would believe women to be a soft touch. We went away for the weekend.

On Monday afternoon I entered the playground and was

met by the woman who had looked after my children. 'You should have been here this weekend,' she said. I asked her why. 'He came with an older woman. They sat here all day Saturday and all day Sunday. I think they were waiting for you, but you never came.'

Susy Brooke

Boy's own adventure

I'd pestered my dad for ages to let me take our weekly trip to my aunt's house on my own. After all, I was now eight and I knew where to get on and off the bus. He eventually agreed to meet me there later, and we would return home together.

So there I was on the bus, looking out of the window as the houses flashed by, feeling all grown up. I was so wrapped up in my thoughts about the future that I didn't notice the bus passing my intended stop. When it dawned on me, I jumped up in panic and begged the conductor to let me off. But he wouldn't until we reached the next stop. I stared wildly out of the window looking at places I didn't recognise, willing the bus to hurry up and get there.

When it finally did, I tumbled out and started to run back the way we had come, desperately trying to remember the corners the bus had turned, not knowing how far we had travelled past my aunt's house. My heart was pounding, not with exertion but fear. I was sobbing. Images of being lost for ever and of never seeing my family again flew through my head. I started praying that if God would just see to it that I got back safely, I would always be a good boy, never talk back to my dad, not tease my brothers and sister, and most of all I wouldn't play around in Sunday school.

After what seemed an eternity I eventually recognised where I was and made my way to my aunt's. By the time I arrived the fear had subsided, together with my promises to God.

Thirty years later at a family gathering, we started reminiscing. We began by telling each other stories of near misses and escapades, before moving on to admissions of past secrets. This was one story I'd never told. Even though, as I'd grown older, I'd worked out for myself that the bus had only run past my stop by a few hundred yards, the memory of the fear had never left me.

When I finished my tale and everyone had laughed at my innocence, my father said, 'I know, son.' I was astounded, and asked him how. He told me that even though I'd thought that I was grown up at eight, I had still been his little boy. When I had left to catch the bus, he had taken his bicycle and, following another route, reached the bus stop before me. He'd watched me get on to the bus and then cycled to the stop I should have jumped off at. When I didn't, he'd set off in pursuit of the bus. He admitted he'd hidden when I came running round the corner, crying my eyes out. I asked him why he hadn't come to me. He told me that he knew I was safe but that he'd been there just in case. One day he wouldn't, and I needed to learn to cope.

Francis Wood

the grim reepo

'Poinding' is a Scottish word. It's used in Scottish law and means to impound a person's goods. If you haven't paid your bills, the solicitors will send men in black suits to poind your things. They walk through the house poinding. Table and chairs: £50; television set: £80; wardrobe: £30; pictures on the wall: £150. They make a list of what they want to auction and come back later to pick them up. Once your goods have been poinded you cannot move or sell them. If you're out when the men come back, they can force entry and take what they've poinded.

In the early 1990s we lived in a house in Edinburgh. Along with tens of thousands of others my parents' house was in negative equity. When my parents couldn't suffer the crippling interest rates any more, the mortgage repayments slipped and within six months we were homeless. We weren't on the street, but it was homeless enough – shunting from a borrowed basement flat to various rented places.

The mortgage company sold the house for £40,000 less than the mortgage was worth, which meant my parents no longer had a house but still had massive debts. I think it was about a year after the house had been repossessed that we were in our second rented flat. By this time the family unit was straining at the seams. With unmanageable debt there is no room for manoeuvre and there is no breathing space; you feel like you are drowning in debt. I suppose my father was pushed to some sort of breaking-point because he ignored everything: electricity bills went unpaid; the rent was missed; envelopes were never opened. Eventually they came and poinded the lot in the name of my father's debt, telling us they'd be back in a month to take it all away. And that was when my mother, who until then had been passive and confused, took her first step towards control.

The poind list was comprehensive and covered four sides of A4. My mother went through it, item by item, and then engaged a lawyer recommended by a friend. A week later we went back with our own completed list which detailed the origin and ownership of everything noted on their list. My mother had written, 'Small silver mouse – this was a wedding present from my mother to me. Table – I bought this in Cheshire, our first house. Antique clock – a gift from my aunt. Mahogany desk – this belongs to my eldest son.' And so on until it was proved that my father owned nearly nothing. The thing was, it was true. The lawyer couldn't promise anything, but she would try.

The day arrived when the bailiffs were due to come. They'd sent a letter asking us to be in at 1 p.m. My father had gone out and my mother and I sat among her belongings and furniture in the flat in Leith. We watched my grandfather's clock tick down the minutes until the walls were closing in.

'Shall we sit in the car?' I said to my mum. So we took tea and digestives across the road to sit in her pale blue Metro, and we waited for the men in black to arrive. We watched through the rear-view mirror. A little after one o'clock two men appeared, walking down the street. They stopped at our house and checked their notes.

'My God, they're here,' said my mum as they knocked on the door. Suddenly we felt foolish, hiding in the car.

'Wait,' I said, 'they're going away.' They turned towards us and through the folds of their coat we saw a flash of gold. Bibles. They were Jehovah's Witnesses. My God. They left and no one took their place. We looked at each other and burst out laughing. My mum smiled like she used to and, for a moment, she could breathe.

Ed Ewing

Brain of Britain

My father always liked to ask questions. It was not that he didn't know the answers, but that he wanted to make sure we knew the answers, too. Nor did he confine his questions to the family. I'm told that the staff in the hospital where he was a surgeon quaked in their shoes when they realised that my father was to perform an operation on a particular day, and that they were to be on duty with him. During long complex sessions (perhaps a heart operation) he kept the theatre staff on their toes by firing general knowledge questions at them. If they didn't know the answers – and they often didn't – they were sent out of the room to telephone the information department of the local city library and find the answers. In those days before mobile phones there must have been much coming and going in the operating theatre.

He could often seem quite ferocious. His mother was

Spanish and he had inherited her dark eyes and thick eyebrows which he would use effectively. We were never allowed to answer, 'I don't know.' We would be pointed in the direction of a dictionary, atlas or encyclopaedia and be expected to look up the answer – the idea being that we always remembered better a fact we had researched ourselves.

Sunday high tea was the time that we children dreaded most. Seated around the large kitchen table, hoping to look invisible, we would be filled with apprehension about the subject of the day. He would often start with the dates of the English kings and queens. Then he might move on to famous battles, or foreign kings and queens. But his main interest lay with world capitals. And there were so many of them. Having mastered Europe (an easier task when the Soviet Union was still one large, single country) he progressed to Africa. On the way we might be quizzed on the islands in between – the Canaries (Santa Cruz) or the Cape Verde islands (Praia). Then it would be all the world's islands, large or small. (I had problems with Madagascar and Greenland and all the tiny islands of the Dutch Antilles.) Once we reached the mainland of South America I felt more confident – Brazil took up so much space and there were only twelve other countries to learn about. No one who came to our house was immune: elderly grandmothers, au pairs, even school friends hoped not to catch my father's eye.

One weekend some distant relatives came to stay. There were four of them – children aged two and eight and their parents. On the Sunday we all sat around the (dining-room, this time) table with the two-year-old seated in a highchair. I realised too late that they hadn't been warned about what might happen, and my father had just reached Asia. I was sitting on my father's right and had calculated that, if he proceeded clockwise, he would come to me last. I was worrying about the capital of China – there seemed to be several choices on the atlas – but his question took me by surprise. 'What is the capital of Outer Mongolia?' he asked.

There was just the barest of pauses and then came the small, clear voice from the two-year-old in the highchair across the room. 'Ulan Bator,' he said.

Jill Simmons

Mother love

I didn't find out that I was adopted; I always knew. Mum and Dad must have talked about my 'other mummy and daddy' so often that by the time I was able to understand what adoption meant I had already absorbed all the relevant facts through a kind of osmosis. In fact, I felt special. I imagined a baby shop, full of bawling infants, price-tags attached, and Mum and Dad coming in, spotting me and saying, 'We'll have that one, please.'

I was curious about my natural mother, of course. I would sometimes fantasise about bumping into her on a crowded street and both of us knowing, in that one instant, that we were mother and daughter. But for most of the time I thought about my adoption in quite a detached way, because I was a happy, contented child. I felt that I belonged where I was.

It was Mum who watched a television show on adoption

in the late 1980s, and was so moved by the plight of the women featured in it that she suggested we try to contact my natural mother to let her know I was 'all right'. In retrospect, it was an act of incredible selflessness on Mum's part.

We contacted the adoption agency soon afterwards and, amazingly, struck lucky. My natural mother had phoned them, less than a month earlier, to leave her new telephone number and address – and instructions to call her if I ever got in touch.

I chose the Royal Festival Hall as the setting for our reunion and asked Mum to come with me as far as Waterloo station. I was petrified about the meeting ahead, but Mum's strength and conviction bolstered my own.

As I was leaving the station I looked back at Mum, a small white-headed figure, sitting in the platform coffee bar, and, despite everything, I felt like a deserter.

I walked down to the basement gallery at the Festival Hall, my palms wet with fear. There was only one other person there, a small blonde woman, about forty years old, who was wandering around the exhibit. After a few minutes I realised that she must be the one. We were surreptitiously glancing at each other, and there was no one else around. For a moment I lingered in the no-man's land between the past and future. I knew I could still walk away, even now, without a backward glance. But if I chose to stay, everything would be changed.

Our reunion was exciting and emotional, the words tumbling out in a heady rush to fill the spaces left by the last twenty years. And we were, strangely enough, instantly familiar. In conversation we danced laterally from one subject to another with complete ease and it felt like the beginning of a great love affair.

We left the Festival Hall and walked past the Thames in the bright August sunshine. After some time I looked at my watch and, realising how late it had got, said that I must go. Thinking guiltily of Mum waiting for me all this time, I broke into a sprint and ran the half mile back to Waterloo station.

I was hot and breathless when I arrived, and, as the platform loomed into view, I thought perhaps Mum had given up and gone home. But there she was, dear and familiar, sitting just where I had left her all that time ago. And, in that moment of relief and gratitude, I suddenly understood about the love of a mother for her child.

Hannah Moruzzi

A best case

The doctor looked at me with an expression of total disbelief.

'Pretending?' he said, incredulously. 'Your little girl has a very serious deficiency in her hearing, very serious indeed. I am, quite frankly, absolutely astonished that you haven't noticed this before now. She must be missing a great deal of school because, with this degree of hearing loss, she won't be able to make out very much at all in the classroom.'

'But . . .' I protested weakly, 'she can hear a chocolate wrapper at five hundred yards. She must be pretending.' The doctor's face now displayed real dislike, mingled with contempt. 'Your daughter has failed this hearing test three times, twice with the school nurse and once here at this clinic with me. She has always failed on the same frequencies and, let me assure you, a 5-year-old child most certainly could not pretend to do that.'

I was stunned and also rather ashamed, as the doctor had obviously intended. He told me that he would refer Sarah to hospital for assessment by a surgeon and that, in the meantime, I should advise her teacher that she would need extra support in class.

On the way home, I guiltily asked her if she'd like an ice-cream and she innocently asked me to repeat what I'd said. I felt terrible. The next day, I spoke privately to the teacher, who was very surprised. She hadn't noticed any problems with the child's hearing and said that, far from missing a lot of school, she was easily the brightest and most active member of the class.

Now I had a real problem. If Sarah genuinely did need surgery, she obviously had to have it and I didn't want to scare her. If, on the other hand, she was somehow cleverly pretending, I had to try to persuade her to pass the hospital hearing test.

Inspiration came when she told me how much she was looking forward to learning to swim during the holidays. I explained that if she had to have an operation on her ears, while it would be great fun in the children's ward and she'd have a lovely stay in hospital, she wouldn't be allowed to swim for quite a long time afterwards. She was mildly disappointed, but not exactly devastated. However, luck stayed with me and the night before our appointment at the hospital, she wandered in to watch television just as a news story about pioneering back surgery popped up, complete with a clip of an operation. 'What's that?' exclaimed Sarah. 'That's an operation,' replied her father, without thinking.

'*That* is an operation?' whispered the horrified child. I could almost hear the cog-wheels turning in her head. Next day, on the way to the hospital, I casually mentioned that if she failed the hearing test, they would have to do lots more tests, which would probably take up most of the day. If she passed first time, well, then there just might be time to go to McDonald's on the way home. She was with the consultant, on her own, for an anxious twenty minutes, but the diagnosis was straightforward. Perfect hearing! In the car I asked her why she had pretended to be deaf. She stopped stuffing down her Chicken McNuggets for long enough to look ashamed. 'I wanted a hearing aid, like Granddad,' she murmured. 'So that I could switch off my sister.'

Ruth Mackie

Cave alarum

In January 1973 I moved into an army quarter in Penicuik, Midlothian, while my husband was on a four-month tour of duty in Northern Ireland. Some weeks later, after visiting my sister-in-law and her husband in Glasgow, I drove back home along the motorway towards Edinburgh in the darkness with my 2-year-old daughter, Kaye, strapped into a baby seat in the back and my 7-month-old daughter, Shirley, in her carrycot on the front seat – there were no special seats for small babies in those days. The car was a Triumph Vitesse convertible – my husband's pride and joy. The journey was suddenly interrupted by a loud bang, at which point Kaye began screaming in terror. My first thought was that I had had a puncture and I pulled over on to the hard shoulder. Another motorist had heard the same noise and he pulled up in front of me, came round to my door and asked if I'd had a puncture. He then checked my tyres and said all appeared to be well, but he was bewildered as to what had caused the noise. All the while Kaye continued to scream, though I could see no reason for it. I tried to reassure her, with little success, and we set off again. By the time we reached home at 10 p.m., Kaye had cried herself to sleep.

She had been wearing a red all-in-one suit with a hood, and as I carried her into the hallway, I was horrified to discover that the hood was stuck to her head with caked, dried blood. Washing away the blood revealed a nasty wound on the top of her head, just back from her forehead. I froze with terror, having absolutely no understanding of how it had happened. I had not registered with a doctor, having lived in Penicuik for just six weeks, so trawled through the telephone directory, heart pounding, and found the number of a surgery in the village.

I blurted out my strange story to the doctor on call, telling him that I had no idea how my daughter came to be injured. His response was cold and unsympathetic, his main concern being that I had not previously registered with a surgery. He did not come to the house to examine Kaye but told me to give her an aspirin and put her to bed.

Shortly afterwards my husband rang from Belfast. On hearing the story, he asked me to look round the car and check for bullet holes. This was a time when the IRA was extending its terror tactics to bases in Britain; not only service personnel, but also their families were considered at risk. I followed his instructions, and sure enough, inches from where Kaye's head had been, was a tiny hole in the fabric of the car's hood.

The following morning Kaye was back to her normal self. My husband had contacted the local police who arrived to search the car. They uncovered an air-rifle pellet inside Shirley's carrycot. It had ricocheted off Kaye's head and landed beside Shirley in the front seat. The culprits had not been the IRA but teenagers taking pot shots at cars from a motorway bridge.

If the pellet had been a couple of inches lower, it would have entered Kaye's eye and gone straight through her brain. She suffered no long-term ill effects, though she still has a scar on her head, just beyond her hairline.

Sheila Cantlay

Hard labour

I was awakened in the early hours by the first of the pains that I had been awaiting for nine months. It was 1 June 1962 and a fine summer morning. By 7 a.m. I knew that it was time to set off on the twelve-mile journey to hospital to await the delivery. The pains were not frequent but, as this was a first, I thought I would feel happier being in the right place at the right time.

The first indignity was an enema, after which I was told to have a bath and to time my contractions; in those days a cigarette was also allowed. I was glad to have a little time to consider the life-changing experience that was imminent and, by all accounts, very painful. I had absolutely no idea what to expect, and it was too late to find out now – the days of scans, relaxation classes and information packs were yet to come. At that time, at least in my case, antenatal care consisted of being advised to wear flat shoes, and a maternity smock to hide the bump, and attending a monthly clinic to be weighed, have my blood-pressure taken and be prescribed iron tablets. So I went into what I could only assume was full labour totally ignorant of what was to follow. I soon found out, though. The pain was like no other I had ever experienced and seemed to be never-ending. I was informed that I was to be delivered while on my back; I had not even considered that any other position would be available. The pain, breathing and panting continued for six hours until, at 3 p.m., I was allowed to push at will, the final push delivering a 7lb 8oz healthy boy with no stitches required – something else that I had not thought about.

A bottle feeder myself, I joined a ward of three breast-feeding mothers, and it soon became obvious that this fact was duly noted and held against me by the nursing staff, who obviously perceived me as an unfit mother.

Fortunately, the baby did not seem to object to bottle feeding and took to it with gusto. I secretly took a little pleasure in listening to the other mothers complaining of sore nipples, while creeping around the ward in the agony of their stitches.

I had expected to remain in the hospital for the recommended ten days, but on the fourth day a nurse breezed in and, as she wheeled away my baby, informed me with scarcely concealed glee, 'As you are not keeping your baby, we would like you to leave as we need the bed.'

I was numb; I had not expected the sheer brutality of those words. I knew it was to be, but this was too soon. I drew the curtains around my bed, dressed and gathered together my few belongings. Miraculously, the other mothers – all married – had, knowing the situation, disappeared.

I walked down the corridor with tears cascading down my cheeks. I reached the nursery and took one last look at my baby, held his hand, said goodbye and left the hospital. Still sobbing, I walked into the town, caught a bus and went home with an empty heart to an equally empty house.

Celia Henderson

In the Line of Duty

Buy the book

My introduction to the world of direct selling came in 1956 with a job peddling sets of encyclopaedias door to door in northern working-class areas at nineteen guineas the set. No appointment, no previous contact with the customer, just 'cold calling'. A knock on the front door and may the best man win! In terms of difficulty and sales resistance the job was without equal, and to call it a baptism of fire in selling was a monumental under-statement. The drop-out rate for reps was phenomenal, many not lasting a single week. However, the few, the very few, who could handle it usually went on to do great things in selling. In short, it required not only salesman-ship of the very highest calibre, but the skin of a bull rhinoceros as well. After a hard day's work in a textile mill the average punter was not particularly thrilled at the prospect of listening to a desperate salesman pitching his spiel as an evening's entertainment.

Thus it was then, that a freezing November night that winter found me working my miserable way through driving sleet in the back streets of Rochdale, giving my all to the task of completing my weekly quota of orders. I was saturated and chilled to the bone. Needing just one final signature to hit my target, I squared my shoulders as my knock on the door was answered by a pinny-ed and curler-ed apparition. Her response to my introductory spiel was, 'Yer'll 'ave ter tork ter 'im.'

She led me through to a tiny back kitchen where a red-headed colossus in workshirt and braces was making steady inroads into the biggest plate of fish and chips I had ever seen. A pint bottle of beer stood at his elbow and at that moment I would have killed to exchange situations.

As any experienced salesman will confirm, it is not the 'prospect' who contradicts or argues with everything one says who is the rep's nightmare, nor is it the one who is difficult to bring to a 'closing' situation. No! – the worst thing of all is the totally unresponsive type, the man who offers no reaction whatever, negative or positive, to anything one says, and in this category Ginger was the archetype. Not only did he not utter a single syllable as I prattled through my sales pitch, but he didn't even deign to look at me, his gaze never shifting a centimetre from that half acre of haddock and chips which, as I desperately pitched on, he conveyed from plate to palate with the monotonous rhythm of an automaton.

I was reminded graphically of the Arctic conditions outside as the melting sleet from the back of my hair ran under my collar and down my back, and I redoubled my efforts, telling myself he would have to shoot me before I left that house without an order. All to no avail! I threw everything at him, every last sales trick in the book. Nothing! Not a word, not a glance. At this point, with the heaviest of hearts, I finally decided to call it a day. As I closed my briefcase I thought, 'If I take nothing else away, I'll take a laugh.' I moved closer to the kitchen table and declaimed in tones of ringing sincerity, 'Do you realise, sir, that these volumes even contain the fullest possible account of the lesser-known traits of the Northern tribes of the Hindu Kush!'

He laid down his knife and fork, and for the first time since I entered the room he looked me in the eye and, miracle of miracles, he spoke. 'Reight, lad,' he said, 'We'd better 'ave 'em.'

Bryan Owram

Joyrider

Late one night my husband and I were woken by the telephone ringing. A worried woman wanting the doctor – my husband – to call and see her ill child. Still half asleep my husband pulled on his trousers and sweater over his pyjamas, went out into the cold night air, and drove away. The address of the semi-detached house was at the end of a cul-de-sac on a large council estate just about 1½ miles away. On arrival at the house he was greeted by the child's mother and taken upstairs where he examined the feverish little girl. He reassured her mother all was well, then gave her advice about treatment.

On leaving the patient's home my husband's beautiful green Ford Zodiac was nowhere to be seen, nor was it in the nearby streets. The police were contacted and arrived quickly. The inspector wanted a detailed description of the missing car, and then as he kindly drove my husband home, said: 'Don't worry, your car will be returned to you as all neighbouring forces will soon know of its disappearance.'

A hot cup of tea was most welcome after an unusually long time away from home on a night call; but no more sleep was had that night. We wondered how my husband's work could be carried out without a car: in those days lots of house calls were made. At 3 a.m. the telephone rang, and a police officer from a neighbouring force wondered if my husband would be willing to examine one of his regular patients, Mr X, who had been taken into custody suspected of being drunk in charge of a vehicle on the seafront. The officer then changed his mind and said it would probably be better if the police surgeon examined Mr X, as his final conclusion as to the state of his health would be impartial. This alternative having been agreed upon, my husband informed him that, in any case, he was without transport. 'By the way, what was the detainee driving?'

'Hang on,' said the policeman, and shortly afterwards: 'A green Ford Zodiac.' We were thrilled and grateful, and especially pleased that the car had not been damaged. Mr X had been drinking in a pub the night before, found an unlocked car, and travelled about five miles to enjoy the sea view!

At 8.45 a.m. my husband parked as usual outside his surgery, and as he was unlocking the surgery door, he was confronted by Mr X waiting to enter the premises. He said he would be most grateful if he could please have a sick note as he was not feeling too grand, and he thought a few days not working would do him good. He never even glanced at the car he had commandeered the night before, and seemed oblivious of the fact it was to his own doctor that he had caused so much upset and worry. And would you believe it, my dear husband did not say a word.

Joan Bell

Maiden voyage

My new boss was a good man. He'd just given me a job as his personal assistant even though I'd confessed I was a bad speller, my typing was slow and my shorthand rusty (which was an overstatement; it was almost non-existent). I told him that I really needed the job because my husband was unemployed and we had a mortgage.

'Well, Girl,' he said (I didn't mind his manner of addressing me, feminism not being an issue then in Newcastle). 'You've been honest with me, and I'll be straight with you. I really need a PA urgently. Get the dictation down as best you can so long as you catch my meaning. Type the letters slowly – you'll get faster. And check the spelling – there's a dictionary on that shelf. Bring the letters to me to sign and if they're not right, you'll just have to do them again. You can start tomorrow. Oh, and by

the way, I like to begin early. Be here at eight o'clock.'
Luckily it suited me fine to be at work at that time.

My boss ran an engineering firm. He was in and out of
the workplace all day, his white shirtsleeves rolled up above
his elbows, and usually in need of a wash when he came to
check up on me and sign letters. As time went on he
dictated less, simply telling me to write to so-and-so with a
piece of my mind, politely. When there was a problem he'd
ask me what I thought and I'd venture a suggestion. He'd
knock it about a bit and come up with another solution.
'OK,' I'd say. 'You're the boss.'

After that I called him simply 'Boss' and he called me
'Girl'. I made him tea, ran his errands and even drove him
to meetings in Newcastle. During one of these trips he said,
'You'd better have a firm's car. The last one did, and your
typing's got better.' He had an easy-going relationship with
all the staff but we knew our place and gave our all when
needed. The yard was working full tilt to get a North Sea oil
platform ready on schedule. Through the windows we could
see the monster as it grew outside on the quay, and we all
took pride in her. (I'm sure that, like a ship, she was female.)
There were setbacks, of course, and Boss shouted and
chivvied and fussed like an old hen, and we all ran about
doing his bidding. Completion was set for October and
during a fine autumn the work on the rig was making good
progress – until the gales came, ruffling the surface of the
Tyne.

One morning I drove to work through a rainstorm,
parked the car in the lee of a shed and was ready for dictation

just before eight o'clock. 'You're on time, Girl, despite the awful weather. Get me a cup of tea and we'll make a start. I've been here all night.' I put a mug of hot, strong tea on the desk in front of him, sat down opposite him with my back to the window and started to take dictation. My own brand of shorthand was going quite well and I scarcely looked up when he paused. The silence lengthened, drawing out further and further. I raised my head. He was transfixed; his mouth was open, his jaw moving, but no sound came. His eyes were wide-open in horror.

'Boss, sir, what's the matter? Are you ill?' I rushed round to his side of the desk to attempt to resuscitate him and then I saw what he saw: the rig moving slowly and majestically past the window, down the Tyne. There was no sound except for the wind and rain battering the windows. The men on the quayside seemed to turn to stone. Only the rig moved.

Joy Harman

Sleeping on the job

Paddy's appearance gave the impression he was a man of the cloth, with his black coat and trousers. His clothes were threadbare; there was little he could do about the fraying around the collar and cuffs of his coat, but he always tried to ensure his white shirt was clean. The black cap he wore at a rakish angle was greasy with wear. It was obvious that his shoes let the water in. Life had not been easy for Paddy since leaving Ireland.

Each morning, Paddy – with bunches of parsley tucked into the crook of his arm, and the remainder in a sack slung across the shoulder of the other – would stand opposite Billingsgate fishmarket, outside the post office at the bottom of St Mary's Hill. In the years after the war I was in my teens, and working in the market as an 'empty boy', or porter.

Paddy would try to catch the eye of the buyers as they

left the market, and sell them bunches of parsley for sixpence a bunch. People acknowledged him as they passed, as he was well known locally and most had an affectionate spot for him, especially the market's fish porters.

All around him people would be pushing and shoving, shouting 'Mind your backs'. It was as if the people surrounding him were like ants, on maniac runs, all trying to get wherever they were going before the other fellow. The noise was enormous: the clatter of horses' hoofs, the thunder of the iron-tiered wheels of the carts and trolleys as they rumbled over the granite-cobbled sets, wet with slippery ice and fish slime.

When business was slow, Paddy would step off the pavement into the road and walk the streets and alleyways, which formed a part of the market, to try to sell his parsley. Horse and carts would clatter by laden with tea chests brim full of live crabs and lobsters all trying to escape. Stacked high were sack upon sack of cockles and mussels, winkles, oysters and scallops. Porters hurtled by with their barrows laden with boxes of fish.

It was frequently when threading his way through this mayhem that Paddy's eyelids would start to grow heavy, and knowing there was nothing he could do about it, he fell asleep where he stood, often in the middle of the road.

Paddy suffered from 'Sleepy Sickness Plague' (*Elicephalton Lethargica*), a disease which has now died out. Some sufferers would fall into a deep sleep never to wake up again, others like Paddy suffered from continuous periods of suspended animation. No one ever knew the cause; some said it was a virus, others that it was caused by the bite of the tsetse fly.

With Paddy standing there, fast asleep, the most amazing thing would happen: the whole world of hustle and bustle which was Billingsgate Market would move around him. Porters swerved to miss him. The drivers of the horse and carts steered their teams of horses around him. Lorry drivers gave him a wide berth. While Paddy stood in the trance, it was quite normal for people to walk up to him and serve themselves by taking a bunch of parsley from his arm, and slipping a sixpence into his coat pocket.

After about five minutes Paddy would awaken, count the bunches of parsley missing from the crook of his arm, and check the sixpences in his pocket. It was very rare for anyone to take advantage of him. Hitching his sack he would continue on his way, as if nothing had happened.

Ron Taylor

Bedside manners

My first experience as a volunteer nurse overseas was when I was asked to help resurrect a dilapidated hospital in Ghana. I had never been to Africa before and had no idea what I would be expected to do.

The hospital itself was built on the top of a very steep hill. It was constructed by the British, who presumably thought the mosquitoes couldn't fly that high and that the local villagers enjoyed a gradient of one in four to get medical treatment.

The building was in a state of total disrepair and had not been used for some years. There was no electricity and no water so every undertaking presented a real challenge. However, myself and the Administrator, who had also come from England, set to with the enthusiasm of novices. After a few months we opened the doors of the hospital to the local people. We did not have a doctor but several dedicated Ghanaian nurses and midwives. I was the boss lady and armed with my bible, a book called *Where There is No Doctor*, I saw between sixty to ninety patients daily.

Eventually the in-patients' ward was repaired and we could admit women and children. The beds had been built, the walls painted, and mosquito netting put on the windows. Against the advice of the nurses I bought pillows and sheets: I was told the sheets would be stolen within the first month, but I wanted the place to look really welcoming. The nurses were right, within a few weeks we had no sheets in the hospital but many of the washing lines in the village boasted flapping white squares.

A male nurse was employed to undertake night duty and after a couple of weeks I decided to check on his work as each morning his report was always the same: 'All the patients slept well'. I found it difficult to believe that in this frantically busy hospital no one ever stirred at night. I rose from my bed about midnight and, torch in hand, walked from my quarters across to the ward. I shone my torch through the window and to my horror every bed bar one was empty. Had the patients all run away? I walked up to the one occupied bed and shone my torch into the face of the heavily sleeping night nurse. When I finally woke him I asked where all the patients had gone. He sleepily replied they were all fine and he shone my torch on to the floor area.

To my surprise the whole ground was full of bodies. Patients, children, husbands, wives and for all I knew, uncles, aunts and cousins, all sleeping peacefully under the beds. Apparently my lovely beds were far too dangerous to sleep in. An understandable assumption if they were to be occupied by a whole family! In their own houses the families slept together on mats on the floor and that was exactly what they intended to do in the hospital. When dawn broke the relatives would pack up their belongings and disappear down the hill back to their homes, and the patients would return to their high beds in time for the white Sister with her strange Western ideas to do her rounds.

Judith Eiloart

Dinner date

My husband Jeremy is a very clumsy man. He is six feet three inches tall, and quite a reasonable width, and has simply no idea of the space he takes up. I believe it is a hereditary disorder as all three of our children are equally afflicted, and throughout the day and night they can be heard ricocheting off the walls of our house.

Many of our friends have lived to regret their choice of cream or beige carpet, particularly when taking into account that Jeremy will always prefer to drink black coffee, or red wine. They are usually prepared to forgive him though, as he is able to provide them with an arsenal of amusing stories that can warm up any flagging dinner party.

Gerry is my oldest friend. She is also one of the most elegant women I know, always impeccably dressed. In fact, an evening out with Gerry and her husband is preceded by frantic activity from my dressing-room as I try on every item of clothing I possess. I will always feel a frump next to Gerry.

Gerry has a superbly forgiving sense of humour, which has been put to the test on many occasions when seated next to Jeremy at the dinner table. On a particularly memorable evening, Jeremy and I were dining out with Gerry and her husband at a country pub. It was a glorious evening, with the sun just beginning to fade as we drove off into the Lancashire hills. Unfortunately, Jeremy's driving skills reflect his difficulties with coordination, and as we spilled out of the car, we were all a little unsteady on our feet.

Having bought some drinks at the bar – my husband had chosen a pint of beer rather than his usual glass of red – we went straight to the restaurant, a rather chic affair, resplendent with white tableclothes and crystal glasses. My only disappointment, I would have to say, was a lack of music. It was so quiet it was almost funereal. Everyone was whispering to each other, and from time to time there was an uncomfortable silence. We were seated at a long, narrow table. Gerry sensibly chose to sit opposite Jeremy, with the full length of the table between them; her husband and I faced each other across the width.

We began to find talking in a whisper was putting a strain on the conversation and had sunk into silence when the waiter arrived with the starters. Jeremy pronounced his soup delicious, and felt the urge to toast the excellent food, raising his pint of beer high into the air. I believe I knew what was about to happen a split-second before the beer glass slid smoothly through Jeremy's fingers into his almost full plate of soup. Glass and plate glided effortlessly across the length of the table, and I just managed to glimpse the look of horror on Gerry's face as both spilled forth their contents on to her cream trouser-suited lap.

As Gerry screamed the entire bistro was on its feet in disbelief. The waiter, who barely batted an eye at the commotion, leaned in towards a stunned Jeremy and said, 'I believe you got away with that one, sir. I don't think anyone has noticed.'

Fran Adelman

Inspecting the troops

In September 1939 we were evacuated from our school in the Midlands to a grammar school in a small market town in Gloucestershire. One Sunday morning in early summer, just after my fourteenth birthday, my friend and I decided we would go to the Methodist church to hear our geography teacher, Mr Jenkins, preach. We could never really understand what his message was because we didn't listen to him properly, but we did like the way he spoke so fervently, waving his arms about and letting his hair fall over his glasses.

The wide high street was almost deserted as we walked down towards the market cross. There we saw a group of about twenty soldiers standing on the pavement near an army lorry. They were not like soldiers we had seen before, upright and smart, so we stopped to watch them. They were bedraggled and untidy, their uniforms dirty. They didn't even appear to be properly dressed. Few wore caps; some were in battledress, and some were only in shirts which were mostly torn and buttonless; their boots were cracked and grey. We noticed two men weren't wearing boots at all but had rags wrapped round and round their feet. They stood about smoking, shoulders hunched. They hardly spoke at all, and looked exhausted. We wondered if they had been on some exercise. Whatever it had been, it must have been hard for them to get into such a state.

After a few minutes a large black car stopped near the group and a lady stepped out. We immediately recognised Queen Mary. She was dressed completely in white: her toque (the kind of hat she always wore), her long dress and gloves, her shoes and even her stockings – all were spotless white. She was a picture of elegance.

As she moved towards the group of soldiers, the contrast could not have been greater. Their sergeant stood to attention and saluted as his men shuffled along the pavement. She walked slowly along the line, her back straight as a board. They did not stand properly or bow or salute as we expected them to. Some looked directly into her pale, set face as she spoke to each of them. Others did not even lift their heads, but stood downcast with their shoulders sagging. Not one of them looked pleased to see her, and we couldn't help but notice their apparent disrespect.

After speaking to each of them she returned to her car and was driven away. We hurried to chapel to hear Mr

Jenkins who was as fervent as ever. Several groups of people stood talking in the high street when we came back from the service, but the soldiers had gone. My friend asked a lady why Queen Mary had come to see them.

'They've come from Dunkirk,' she said in a hushed voice. The name meant nothing to us. We ran along the lane to the fields and picked wild flowers.

Barbara Ward

We'd been married for six months and were still living with Mum and Dad when we saw the flat advertised. Maybe because Mrs Grant-Simmons liked the look of us or, more likely, because we were both working in what were then secure jobs, we were selected from several couples to rent a tiny self-contained ground floor flat with its own front door and pocket handkerchief-sized garden for five pounds a week. In grander days the building had been the gardener's lodge and was built adjacent to a Victorian mansion where the elderly Mrs Grant-Simmons occupied the ground floor.

Into the flat we moved our few possessions. Our small savings stretched to carpet, curtains and new oven. It gave us great satisfaction to put the place together. I used my old Singer to make the curtains, and leftover remnants to brighten up the second-hand three-piece. Having studied the complimentary cookery book that came with my oven, which had an automatic timer, we would return from work – after travelling from London for almost two hours in a grimy, draughty British Railways carriage – to the enticing smells of casserole, Lancashire hotpot or roast chicken. I was very anxious to impress my new husband with my cooking prowess, believing that the way to a man's heart was indeed through his stomach. In that little dwelling we dreamed our visions of a bright and promising future. Life seemed uncomplicated. We didn't yearn for dishwashers, freezers or washing machines; a weekly visit to the launderette sufficed, and for the same amount as the rent we could buy provisions for the whole week.

There was such excitement when, after my cousin became apprenticed to a television rental company, he found us a second-hand black and white set for the princely sum of £9. I had momentary regrets for the poor souls who had had theirs repossessed but every cloud has a silver lining and I visualised cosy nights in our first home before a roaring fire watching *Play of the Week* and *Film Night*. Newspapers were henceforth a luxury we could do without as we could be home for the seven o'clock news if our trains ran to time.

I had graduated beyond *Basic Cookery* – Chapter One. Enthused by menus in the staff restaurant at BBC Overseas Broadcasting, where I worked as a young secretary, I had reached Chapter Two – Hungarian goulash, spaghetti bolognaise and the like. Keeping in mind my budget and the oven's pre-timing function I planned a special meal for our first evening's viewing. The set was due the next day.

Before leaving and as per instructions I filled two lean lamb's hearts with a fragrant stuffing, wrapped them in silver foil and placed them on the top shelf. Underneath, I put the ingredients for a rice pudding in a glass dish. I adjusted the timer, offered up a quick, silent prayer to the Saint of All Kitchens and Young Wives and ran to catch my train.

That night we sat before the cumbersome black box. It looked a little incongruous on our small coffee table, but we felt wonderful. The news was beginning as we carried to the table our steaming stuffed hearts, creamy mashed potatoes and carrots. We lifted our knives and forks in mouth-watering anticipation, peering interestedly as a stunning news item flashed on the television screen.

On this early December day in 1967 Christiaan Barnard had performed the first ever heart transplant and the miracle of his handiwork was revealed to us. As well as the graphic description, including magnified pictures, the elated narrator told viewers the intricate details of this historical operation.

I threw the stuffed hearts in the bin untouched. The rice pudding was delicious.

Jean Thomas

the gentleman skinhead

I'd had a day off my work as a primary school teacher feeling unwell, but returned to school the next day as the headmistress had asked me to. I got only as far as the playground, however, as I met the headmistress there.

She took one glance at me and said, 'You look dreadful. Why have you come?'

'Well,' I replied, 'you asked me to come in as soon as possible.'

'But not if you're ill,' she said. 'Go to the doctor now.'

Relieved, I walked the quite considerable distance to the surgery. The doctor gave me a certificate for a few days' absence and I set off to catch a bus home. To reach the bus stop I had to cross the busy main road in Croydon. Using the subway was the quickest way. I wasn't very keen on subways and this was a long and rather dark one. Normally I would have chosen the longer way round and used the traffic lights. But the way I felt meant I would have to take the shorter route that day. My energy was fast running out. So I started off down the slope and made my way through the dim passage.

There had been a great deal of rain over the previous few days, and there must have been something wrong with the drainage in the subway. As I reached the lowest point, just before it turned up to the right to lead out to the bus stops, imagine my dismay as I was confronted with a lake of water. It looked deep, dark and forbidding. There was no way I could walk across it. The water would have reached well over my ankles.

As I stood there, on the brink, I became aware of a group of youths at the other side of the water. They all had their heads shaved in the skinhead fashion. They were laughing and generally making a noise. I must admit it was the sort of group that I would usually go well out of my way to avoid. Just as I was about to turn round to go back the way I'd come, one of the boys came to the edge of his side of the water and called to me. 'Would you like me to carry you across?' I stood transfixed. The boy took a splashing step into the water towards me. He looked at me enquiringly.

I very ungratefully said, 'I know, you'd drop me in the middle.'

'No, I wouldn't,' he replied, 'I've carried others across.'

As I hesitated he waded towards me, the water swirling round his bovver boots. My wary self was telling me to turn about and go the long way round.

My weary self just waited for the boy, who, incidentally, was about the same age as my own two sons. He reached me and I meekly put my arms round his neck. He put one arm under my knees and the other round my waist and lifted me up and began to wade to the other side. Rather embarrassed, halfway over I said, 'I'm not too heavy, am I?' He just grinned. Carefully he set me down on the other side to the noisy amusement of his mates.

I said, 'Thank you – you're a good lad.' He received the first smile of my day and with spirits much uplifted I walked up the slope to my bus stop.

Marguerite Hodgkinson

Blue light district

January in Scotland is normally an exceedingly cold month and 1969 was no exception. Snow lay on the ground and every morning the ritual of scraping the ice off my little Austin A40 meant getting out of a warm bed earlier than I wished. But this particular day was different – I was driving down to Hampshire to see my parents. The A40 did have a heating system but it left a great deal to be desired, so I decided to take some care in choosing my clothes that morning. Anything that had thermal quality was considered, and I bore in mind the advice that layers are better than thickness. On went underpants, followed by a pantygirdle – a fearsome but essential garment of unforgiving elastic that forced any unwanted flesh inwards, so creating the illusion of a trim figure – followed by a pair of old school bloomers, then some thick tights, followed by trousers. I was ready for the journey.

I picked up Anne, a friend who was coming with me, and we set off merrily, with all the necessary goodies to sustain us on the long trip. The journey down through the Borders was uneventful and Anne and I chatted away; but it began to dawn on me that certain portions of my lower abdomen were starting to suffer seriously from inadequate blood supply. I tried loosening some buttons but it soon became apparent that the culprit was the pantygirdle, which had me in a grip from which there was no escape without drastic measures. The traffic was fairly heavy and there were few opportunities to divest myself decently of the offending garment. By now it was absorbing a great deal of my attention and our animated chatter had dwindled considerably. I determined that, as soon as I could, I would simply have to ignore decorum and stop.

The chance did not arrive until we got on to a dual carriageway with a hard shoulder. I pulled over and switched off the engine. Getting out of trousers, tights, bloomers and a stubbornly resisting pantygirdle while sitting at the wheel of a small car is no mean feat, but such was my desperation to escape the clutches of this instrument of torture that I succeeded in record time. As the girdle came down over my knees, I was overwhelmed by a feeling of complete ecstasy. Then the police drove up.

To say I panicked is an understatement; by now I had on only a pair of brief pants. I decided there was only one option: I wound down the window and said, 'Please don't ask me to get out of the car; I had to stop and take my pantygirdle off and now I've only got my knickers on.'

When the officers eventually picked themselves off the bonnet of my car and had wiped away the tears of laughter, they reminded me that stopping on a hard shoulder was not permitted other than in an emergency. I assured them that this was an emergency and, still laughing, they drove away.

My hands shaking, I got back into my clothes and we set off again. As we overtook the police car, cruising in the inside lane, Anne waved the pantygirdle out of the window. The police were good sports – they turned their blue light on.

Rosemary Bowden

Lost forewords

I was working in a little school in the heart of the countryside. It was a two-teacher school and in those days, thirty-five years ago, there were no classroom assistants, just the two teachers, a secretary who came in twice a week to do the dinner money and the post, and a part-timer who took the head's class one afternoon a week.

I'd been working there for a year or so, teaching the Infants – a mixed class of children aged from four to seven, housed in a hutted classroom in the school garden – when the new intake arrived in September. Among them was David Bell, four years old. He came from the next village, and was brought by taxi every day. His father was a farm worker on the local estate and his mother was a quiet, shy woman with three other small children. Apart from on David's first day at school, when his mother came with him, we rarely saw his parents. A younger child was disabled, and the family had to spend a lot of time going back and forth to hospital on the bus, for treatment and physiotherapy.

It soon became clear that there was a problem with David. He just didn't speak. The other children in the class seemed to accept this; there was another little boy who hardly spoke at all either, so David wasn't, at first, outstandingly different. But as time went on his silence became more and more marked. He wouldn't tell his news on a Monday morning; all the others were bursting with it. He didn't ask for anything, and I had to adopt all sorts of strategies in order to guess what he needed. It was possible to teach him; he would play, and use number and reading apparatus correctly; and he even evolved a sign language to indicate the need to visit the lavatories across the playground. His friends helped him; they were his spokesmen, though I never heard him speak to them either. He ate his dinner with quiet concentration. Of course, we didn't leave it there, we called in all the appropriate professionals. His parents weren't too worried; he didn't talk 'much', his mother said, but she was happy for him to see the school doctor, and to have his hearing tested, though this had to be done non-verbally, as for a baby. The speech therapist came, and said that David was an 'elective mute'. She suggested strategies to help but said that, at this early stage, it would be a good idea for him to get on with all the regular work and activities as best he could, and for us to wait for him to be ready to speak.

The year went by. David, dressed as a shepherd, was a

226

gravely silent onlooker at the stable in Bethlehem, and he smiled his way through the Christmas party. He looked, quietly, at everything on the school trip. As the end of the summer term approached, I was getting very worried.

It was a lovely summer. The Infants were able to escape from the hot classroom in the afternoons to use the sand and water in the garden. One Friday David burst through the open door and skidded to a halt by my table. 'Mrs Mundon! There's a dead cat under the classroom!' he panted.

I leapt to my feet. 'David, how wonderful!' I cried.

Then I realised what he'd said. I followed him outside to where the others in his group were lying on their stomachs, peering into the gloomy depths underneath the hut.

He was right.

Rose Mundon

While I was working as a junior reporter on Chelsea's local newspaper, our editor was informed that Harold 'Kim' Philby was holding a press conference at his mother's home in nearby Drayton Gardens that afternoon. It was October 1955 and, at the time, the former Foreign Office official was hot news – Colonel Marcus Lipton MP had just accused Philby of 'dubious third-man activities' in the Burgess-Maclean spy scandal. I was eighteen and, having only just started my job in journalism, was flattered to be assigned to cover the story. 'This "third man" affair is important,' said my editor. 'It will be all over the dailies tomorrow. Try to get something they don't – preferably a local angle.' When I arrived at Drayton Gardens the flat was already packed. There were more than sixty reporters, photographers and film cameramen. Philby, dressed in a dark grey suit, was already surrounded and answering questions.

'Are you the so-called "third man" – yes or no?' asked one reporter.

Philby didn't blink and looked the man straight in the eye. 'I challenge Colonel Lipton to repeat the accusation outside the protection of the House of Commons,' he replied.

Other questions followed: 'How well did you know Burgess?', 'Did you know that Burgess was a Communist?', 'Can you shed any light at all on the mystery?' Philby answered politely and confidently – but no local angle emerged. I noticed that Philby's mother, Dora, an elegant, charming lady, had disappeared from the room. I found her in the kitchen making cucumber sandwiches. I asked her views on the Burgess-Maclean affair.

'I'll be glad when it's all over and Harold can get away for a holiday,' she said. 'We've had some bother with telephone calls and people wanting interviews.' She was friendly and appeared glad to have someone to keep her company. I told her of my predicament. 'Wait until they've all gone,' she said. 'You can join us for tea.'

An hour later the last of the reporters and photographers had left. Philby showed no surprise that I remained. 'This young man is from the local paper, Harold,' said Dora.

Philby ushered me into the main room and fell into an armchair. He closed his eyes, shook his head, took a deep breath and looked over at me standing in the middle of the room. He gestured to a nearby chair. 'How can I help?' he asked. He looked exhausted. He was sweating slightly and his hands were clasped tightly together. I thought it best to get to the point.

'Local angle?' he repeated. 'Well, in 1946 I lived in Chelsea, in Carlyle Square.'

'Did Burgess ever visit you there?'

'Of course. He paid me several visits. At that time we were personal friends.'

'Did you discuss politics?'

'Yes,' he replied. 'But there was nothing to suggest he was communistic in his views. He was all over the place in politics, difficult to get hold of.'

We had our tea and sandwiches and chatted. He said his work in the Foreign Office was a thing of the past and that he had nothing planned for the future. 'I just want peace and quiet for my family and myself. I hope I have cleared the air today. We want to get on with our lives.' As he saw me to the door, his mother wished me luck with the story.

As a parting shot, I asked, 'Are you the "third man" in the Burgess-Maclean affair?'

'My conscience is clear,' said Philby with a smile. 'Besides, do I look like a spy?'

Peter Thipthorp

Radio days

Like every alien living and working in England, I had to have a little grey booklet called an Alien's Registration Book. It showed that I was a Hungarian citizen, born in Budapest, and that I was allowed to enter employment in the United Kingdom. Even when war broke out in September 1939 it made no difference to my status as a 'neutral alien' because Hungary stayed out of the war. But this changed in June 1941 when, as Germany's ally, she took part in the invasion of the Soviet Union and thus became a belligerent. This meant that from being a neutral alien, I became an enemy one.

My wife and I had recently married and we lived in a two-room flat in London. I had known for some time that nearly all enemy aliens – Germans, Austrians and Italians – had been rounded up and sent to internment camps on the

Isle of Man. For days I'd been wondering whether I would also be interned, and when my turn would come. My English wife refused to take the notion seriously and dismissed it with a wave of the hand. 'Of course they wouldn't intern you, the whole idea is ridiculous!' was her attitude. However, I was not so sanguine and was expecting a knock on the door every day. Soon it came. A tall policeman rang our doorbell and said he had come to see me. I invited him into the sitting-room and without further ado he told me that with Hungary's entry into the war I had become an enemy alien and consequently it was his duty to stamp my registration book accordingly. This meant, he explained, that I was not allowed to enter any coastal zone, port or shipyard, any military establishment or munition factory, without the explicit permission of the region's Chief Constable.

From all this I concluded that, apparently, there was no intention of interning me on the Isle of Man after all. Perhaps this was due to the fact that, at the time, I was working in the Hungarian Section of the BBC External Services. However, the officer had not quite finished. Next he asked me if I had a radio. I immediately realised what he was after. Several of my friends and acquaintances in England had been ordered to surrender their radios to their solicitors or hall porters, as, after the fall of France, there was a widespread fear that with a little technical knowledge, a receiving set could be turned into a short-range transmitter with which messages could be passed to spies or enemy agents operating in the neighbourhood. I pointed to our small Philips radio – the only one we owned and which we had received as a wedding present – and told the officer that, yes, indeed, that was the only radio we had.

'I am sorry,' he said, 'but I am afraid that for the duration of the war you will have to hand it over into the custody of a natural-born British subject.'

By this time I was so relieved that I was not going to be interned that I risked a frivolous reply. 'Well, my wife is a natural-born British subject. Could she be handed the radio into her custody?'

The policeman seemed to think hard for a moment or two and then he said, 'All right – but on one condition: only she must switch the radio on or off!'

Ever since that day, although I have been a (naturalised) British subject for well over half a century and, therefore (presumably), out of their direct surveillance, I have had a soft spot for the Aliens Department of the Metropolitan Police.

Francis Rentoul

the apprentice

After perusing my cards and P45, the old foreman nodded. 'All right, lad,' he said. 'You'll do.' Then, standing up behind his wooden desk and stretching his weary back, he trudged across to the office door, motioning me to follow.

As I crossed the Notting Hill building-site that June morning back in the early 1960s, the smell of diesel, cement and wood-shavings filled my nostrils, and my ears echoed with the steady clunk-clunk of a cement mixer. I sniffed the dusty air as the foreman pointed to some men busy unloading a brick-lorry.

'Right, son, you can help those lads over there.' Nodding my thanks, I hitched up my jeans and soon found myself hard at work with a gang of Irishmen. Moisture started seeping from my forehead and running down my dust-smeared face as we grabbed bricks from the lorry – six at a time – and placed them neatly in a stack. As I strove to keep pace with the burly Irishmen, I tried to stem the flow of sweat to my stinging eyes with the back of my hand.

After a while I became aware that the broad-shouldered old chap to my left was acting oddly.

'Here!' I whispered hoarsely to the fella grafting on the other side, flicking my head towards the old boy. 'Is he having a game or what? Look at him! He's only picking up one brick at a time.'

Giving me a meaningful look, the big Irishman I spoke to leant over to me. 'Shh! Say not'ing. Dat's "the Hammer".'

'Yeah! But . . .'

'Didn't you hear me, lad?' The Irishman put his finger to his lips.' Say not'ing!'

Grabbing my six bricks, I threw the old fellow a contemptuous glance. The man glared back so balefully that, mindful of the other chap's warning, I was prudent enough to cast my gaze elsewhere.

When the vehicle had been cleared of its load and the bricks stacked, the driver, who had been hard at work handing us the bricks, produced a broom. After waving goodbye to me and the other men, who were returning to the tasks they'd been busy at before the lorry arrived, he proceeded to sweep the brick dust from the back of the lorry.

I returned to the site office to collect a shovel from the foreman. He pointed to a chap who was digging and told me to go over and help him. To my dismay, as I approached, I could see that the man working on his own was the old

Irishman called 'the Hammer'. Steeling my nerves I jumped smartly into the trench and introduced myself. 'Hi!' I said. 'I'm John!' The man just glared at me. Trying desperately to think of something to say to lighten the situation, I finally asked him why he was called 'the Hammer'.

Whoosh! I never even saw it coming, but suddenly I found myself held fast against the walls of the trench by the man's shovel, the blade of which was piercing my throat.

'And why,' the old chap spat the words out, 'd'you t'ink they call me "the Hammer"?'

'Ugh! Ugh!' I was finding it difficult to speak with the blade of the shovel cutting into my windpipe.

Glaring wildly into my enlarged eyeballs, the Irishman leant unrelentingly on to his shovel. Then in a heavy Dublin accent he yelled, 'It's because I hammer people!'

John Rossiter

A stitch in time

Ready to accept a challenge, I agreed to do the house clearance. A fellow antiques dealer had said it could be a profitable sideline.

Transport from the house in London and storage in our Rutland village would be no problem. My friend Mike owned suitable vehicles and a cavernous barn. We did a reconnaissance of the old terraced house, where we discovered a writing desk that had been forced open and a neighbour who told us the deceased owner had often boasted loudly of having £5,000 hidden in the house for emergencies. The police had apparently tried to find the stash but decided it had been a figment of the woman's imagination. We put two and two together and drew a conclusion that did not include the delusions of an old lady.

The clearance job was just about viable. Mike knew the

ropes. On his advice we took two vehicles. The first and biggest, driven by Mike, was for the valuable items, and the second, driven by his helper, Tim, was for the remainder, the inevitable detritus that would surely include at least one highly toxic old mattress, soiled linen, grease-caked utensils and the useless contents of the bottom of every neglected cupboard and drawer from a lifetime of hoarding.

'There,' said Mike as we roared south on the A1.

'What? Where?' I asked.

'Two skips – see them?' I hadn't but pretended with a nod. 'That's where we dump the rubbish,' said Mike, pressing the truck's horn three times to alert Tim, who later confirmed he'd noticed them.

There proved to be much rubbish among the good stuff, but house clearance means taking everything. Two old and stinking double mattresses in particular had us donning gloves and pinching our noses. They went out of the bedroom window, to go last on the second van. We humped and dumped and filled black bags, and sought the tiniest of valuables. Should we keep the big biscuit-tin of buttons? No. From the drawers of the front bedroom dressing-table we tipped scores of knick-knacks, including a set of dominos, hundreds of fading photographs and, strangely, a sailmaker's needle. We laboured till dusk on that fine summer evening, then headed north with all the rubbish, to be dumped in the two skips provided by someone else's thoughtful council.

The rain had started miles back by the time we reached the lay-by. Hundreds of screaming tyres threw up spray to fog the already darkening road. It served our purpose as pile after pile, armful after armful of debris from the old house went from van to skip with no one to see us. Soaked to the skin, Mike and I made it back to the village and his empty barn in good time. Tim, now the proud owner of the remaining junk, headed home. Mike's partner, Christine, met us and poured hot chocolate down us, then joined in the unloading. She occasionally remarked optimistically, or passed a cautious comment on potential value. As we laboured we took it in turns to regale her with the story of the five grand, the busted-open desk and the police failure to find the stash. She heard of the smelly mattresses and the other junk dumped in the skip and, of course, the peculiar place we found the sailmaker's needle.

'Stop,' she said suddenly. 'Mattresses, sailmaker's needle? *Skip*?'

The journey to the lay-by took an age.

The skips were gone.

Henry Highmore

For the record

My first job on leaving school was in the popular music section of a long-established record store in Newcastle. Late one afternoon I was lolling against the counter, fiddling with a roll of sticky tape, one eye watching the clock. The heavy glass entrance door swept open and in glided a middle-aged gentleman with grey bouffant hair, tinted in pinks and purples around the temples. He sported a green velvet jacket and a cluster of silk scarves and frills. The ensemble was topped off with a wide-brimmed black hat, accessorised with yet another silk scarf, black gloves, and what I would call a swagger stick. And boy, did he swagger; flamboyance oozed from every pore. Today his appearance wouldn't cause a stir, but on that afternoon in the 1970s stirring was in evidence within a 50ft radius, as customers stopped leafing through LP sleeves to gawp.

Until then, I had been under the impression that the world consisted of people exactly like my family and the women I worked with. Conventional people. The expression 'diversity', when applied to the wide spectrum of human beings and their varied appearances, had yet to enter my vocabulary. Suddenly I was confronted with a severe culture shock; I hadn't come across anyone remotely similar to this man before, and I thought he was by far the most exquisite creature I had ever seen.

'My dear,' he said, 'I wish to purchase a recording of Barbara Seville.'

I looked at him with that expression of blank incomprehension so beloved of teenagers. 'Barbara Seville,' I said doubtfully. 'Dunno who she is. Hang on, I'll go and ask somebody.' I sloped off to Classical Music. 'The chap over there' – I indicated my customer with a jerk of the thumb – 'wants something by Barbara Seville. I think she must be an opera singer.'

An inspection of the classical recordings catalogue produced nothing by Barbara Seville, so I returned to the gentleman to elicit further clues. 'What does she sing?' I asked. ''Cos no one's ever heard of her.' My client leant forward to give me a reassuring pat on the hand.

'An easy mistake to make,' he said. 'The Seville to which I refer is not a singer, but in fact *The Barber of Seville* by Rossini. I wish to purchase a version of the work for a friend.'

'Right, I'm sorry. I'll have another look.' At this point a colleague took it upon herself to intervene. She nudged me smartly to one side.

'I'll serve the gentleman,' she barked. 'Out of the way.' I was the junior of the juniors and not in a position to protest, but my effervescent new friend wasn't having any of it.

'The young lady and I are managing perfectly well, thank you, and I'd like her to continue serving me. Kindly leave us alone.' Thus she was summarily dismissed.

'Yeah, shove off!' I muttered inaudibly, my face a picture of satisfaction.

Despite my ineptitude, we together managed to choose a version of Rossini's *Il Barbiere di Siviglia* that fitted the needs of my client. The transaction complete, he replaced his gloves and collected his stick. 'I will wish you good afternoon, my dear, you've been most helpful.'

With that, he departed from my life as stylishly as he had entered it. My gaze followed him as he floated across the shop and out of the door. Emma, the manageress, appeared at my side. 'A most distinctive gentleman,' she said. 'Just imagine, in your dotage you'll be able to tell people about the afternoon you met Quentin Crisp.'

Tammy Linsell

242

Dreamcoat

Charlie Coat was a bloody nuisance. He came into casualty several times every winter, always with the same request: 'I want to come into hospital – me house is cold.' His real name was Charles Simpson but we called him Charlie Coat because he always wore an old khaki gabardine overcoat that was two sizes too big for him, to accommodate the three jumpers and assorted other garments beneath it. He held the front of it together with his arms across his chest, as its lower part flapped about his legs. He had a white beard and was about seventy years old; his coat didn't look much younger. Some years later, when I saw Buster Merryfield, as Uncle Albert in *Only Fools and Horses*, he reminded me of Charlie.

Charlie had once been in hospital with a chest infection and had liked it so much – a warm bed, regular meals, some company and attention – that he kept trying to get back in. The casualty staff regarded people like Charlie as social problems, not the medical cases that a casualty department should be dealing with. He was usually checked over by one of the doctors before being offloaded on to the duty social worker who would have to check that his gas and electricity had not been disconnected again because he hadn't paid his bills.

Like a pub, every hospital has its regulars, on first-name terms with the staff. Some thought that Charlie was just too mean to pay for anything – electricity, gas, razors or a new coat – but I felt sorry for him; it couldn't be that easy living alone on a pension.

The last time I saw him he was his usual self, cheerful and pleasant. I examined him and told him what he already knew: there was nothing wrong with him. We would have to send him home; the hospital was always short of beds, even for patients who were ill.

'OK, Doc,' he said to me, smiling. 'It was worth a try, wasn't it?'

Having been sent home many times before, he didn't seem too disappointed, and I arranged for the social workers to check up on him again. 'Is your gas and electricity on, Charlie?' I asked.

'Oh yes, Doc, I've paid me bills,' he said. I left him smiling and wondered who would have to discharge him from casualty next time, as it was my last week working at that hospital.

Two years later I was back working at the same hospital,

and one afternoon I asked Dave, the charge nurse in casualty, if he still saw Charlie and the other regulars. He mentioned some names that I remembered, but told me that Charlie had gone to the great casualty department in the sky the previous year. He opened the drawer of his desk and handed me a newspaper cutting he had kept there. I saw the headline: LOCAL MAN FOUND DEAD AT HOME.

Underneath, I read that Charles Simpson had been found dead in bed by a neighbour after he hadn't been seen for several days. On top of his bed was an old raincoat with £14,000 in its pockets. I had got married the previous year and taken out a mortgage on a house costing only slightly less than Charlie's hoard. Dave laughed as he said, 'Just think – that's the nearest you and I have ever been to fourteen thousand pounds.'

And Charlie Coat wouldn't be spending it, wherever he was.

Gordon Williams

King of the road

Some of our members may remember him, our temporary coach-driver at the British Limbless Ex-Service Men's Association Home in Crieff, during that long, hot summer a few years back.

Jock was a big bloke, aggressive looking: his back ramrod straight, bulging biceps with snake tattoos, and a T-shirt (when he was wearing one) stretched to busting over his barrel chest. When we arrived at his chosen destination, he would take off his T-shirt to show us some more of his tattoos. He wasn't too old for earrings, either. He had two of them, both in the same ear. One was in the usual place, and its twin was above it in the top rim.

From our seats behind him, Jock's bronzed head looked like a mahogany newel post announcing an impressive staircase. That was the view we had of him as he drove us frantically around on his 'mystery' runs. Sometimes they would begin as a mystery to him, too, since his geography was poor.

One day in Inverary I asked him what he normally did for a living.

'I bounce,' he said.

'Bounce? Trampoline instructor?' I ventured naively.

'Naw,' he said in his broad Glaswegian accent. 'I bounce troublemakers out of a nightclub in Glasgie. See this?' he said, indicating the big brass buckle on the wide belt looped through his tight-fitting jeans. 'When I wrap that round my fist, I mean business. Doonah tangle wi' me, mon,' he said playfully, as he extended alternate fists at me. The sun sparkled on heavy gold rings that could do duty as knuckledusters. Jock's boots – the type worn to shin up Everest – had shiny steel plates encasing the hard toecaps. The heels of this formidable footwear were similarly adorned with decoratively patterned plates that could protect him from a rear attack.

When on duty Jock would be stone-cold sober, he told us, to make sure he had no problems with the hot-headed drunks who tried to cause trouble. Those who were forcibly ejected into the cool night air would actually bounce on the hard pavement outside the club. Jock's fascination with tattoos extended even to his hands. The letters along the top of his fingers read I LOVE YOU. When 'bouncing', Jack gave a dangerously half-drunk clubber no time to read the message, let alone appreciate its irony, before the lights went out.

But Jock was at peace with his passengers. We were all limbless ex-servicemen on holiday and we made him feel whole. Jock counted our heads before setting off on the return journey, to make sure he had everyone on board. If he had divided our arms and legs by four, he would have been a few short. 'All present and correct. No one has escaped,' he would joke.

Jock was very attentive. He was quick to help those on sticks to board the coach, and he carefully loaded and unloaded those of us in wheelchairs using the rear-mounted hydraulic lift, which sometimes had to be encouraged with an armour-plated hoof to withdraw into its hideaway. His time up, Jock said what a pleasure it had been to be with us. 'I'm staying over in Crieff for the car boot sale on Sunday,' he said to me. 'Never know me luck.'

'Looking for something special?' I asked.

'Yee'll nay laff?' he asked diffidently.

(I wouldn't dare.)

'I collect thimbles,' he said.

I couldn't help it: I burst out laughing.

Eric Cottam

the unspoken word

Dicken was a gypsy boy who camped every winter, with his extended family, near Salisbury. Because it was a long stay, he had to go to school and was having problems. He was said to be wild, disobedient, inattentive and difficult to understand. He was referred to speech therapy, and so our paths crossed. Surprisingly, he kept his first appointment. His mother left him at the door, saying she would come back for him. Good as her word, she returned later. Throughout his attendance she never crossed the threshold.

Dicken was a small, wiry child, smelling of wood-smoke, and begrimed by it. He looked inadequately fed and clothed. He was bruised and scratched, but it was impossible to know if these scars were from adventures or chastising. He said he was six years old, but his wary wiliness suggested he was older but undersized. He came

249

compliantly into clinic, went straight to the coal fire, and stood staring into it, his face expressionless. He made no attempt at interaction, yet was clearly aware of everything around him. He volunteered nothing, was reluctant to answer questions, and showed no interest in toys, books or games. Formal testing was impossible. I would have to build trust and confidence through play, and record his spontaneous speech for assessment. He gradually opened up, and sometimes gave a little information about his life. It became obvious that his whole experience, his freedom and values, would make him feel totally alien at school.

His speech difficulty was not severe enough to account for his silence. He substituted some Romany sounds for English ones, and used some unfamiliar words. We worked on these indirectly. He slowly responded to individual attention, and a predictable pattern. He became more biddable, and some interaction emerged. Occasionally he looked as if he had combed his hair before coming, and even smiled shyly, but quite disarmingly. As the weather improved, I guessed his visits would soon stop, abruptly, when the caravan moved on.

One day his behaviour changed. He hung back when we went to our room, was unwilling to turn round, and kept his hands behind his back. He wouldn't play. Breaking my unspoken rule not to question him about himself, I asked, 'Have you hurt your hands, Dicken?' He shook his head. I tried encouraging him to play with something else. Slowly he held out a bunch of daffodils.

'How lovely,' I said. 'Would you like to put them on the table?'

He shook his head.

'Where would you like to put them?' I asked.

'For you,' he mumbled.

'How kind of you, Dicken. Thank you. Did you grow them by your caravan?'

'No,' he answered.

'Did someone give them to you?' He shook his head, and I guessed he had picked them in a garden on the way to the clinic, for they were not wild. I said it was kind of him to bring me a present, and I would take them home to remind me of him. I made no comment on where they came from. If my guess was correct, his mother must have approved, and probably kept watch for him. It seemed more appropriate to value his generous gesture, rather than preach a moral code to a likeable child, who was thoroughly confused by living in a different culture and language. I never saw him again.

Pam Kydd

A date with history

It was a velvety summer's night in 1938 and I lay on a beach in Wellington, New Zealand. My boyfriend was 21-year-old Gordon Saunders, who had been selected to join the Royal Air Force's Empire Air Training Scheme in England. We called them the 'golden boys' and the following year, when war broke out with Germany, they all distinguished themselves by their bravery.

The sky above us was filled with silver paper stars as we lay whispering. Next morning his boat was leaving and we knew these would be our last moments together. We planned how I would come to England the following year and how we would be married in an old country church, just as you see in picture postcards. He also promised that on my arrival he would take me to an RAF mess dinner, wherever he was stationed. The following year war broke out and

Pilot Officer Saunders was posted to No. 87 Squadron. There was no question of my joining him. 'Be patient. It will all be over soon, darling,' he wrote. Unfortunately, Pilot Officer Saunders was shot down in his Hurricane by German fire near Lille in May 1940 and he was posted 'missing, believed dead'. It was several years later that I heard his grave had been found in the French village of Fenain, near the border with Belgium – years that were filled with hope that there had been some awful mistake and that he was waiting for me. In April 1946 I was given passage in the first civilian ship from New Zealand. It was filled with old English ladies coming home to die after being trapped in New Zealand throughout the war.

During the next year I met and married a Danish journalist, Paul von Stemann; so it was not until 1948 that I was able to make my pilgrimage to Fenain. The mayor invited me to visit the village: *'Ah, vous êtes la petite fille dans l'avion,'* was his greeting. Taking my arm he led me to a nearby small museum filled with relics of the war, where I looked at bits of the Hurricane that had been scattered in a field. On the wall above was the miniature of myself that I had given Gordon to celebrate our engagement. He never flew without it.

Fifty-eight years have passed: I am now eighty-seven and live in converted stables in Oxfordshire. One day last autumn while sitting on my verandah I noticed a young man moving into another of the flats in the courtyard. He was wearing the RAF uniform. We waved, and during the next week Flight Lieutenant Barry Todd, an engineer attached to

No. 99 Squadron at RAF Brize Norton, came across and introduced himself. Over the next few weeks we became good friends. I told him that I was interested in the RAF as not only had I hoped to marry an RAF pilot but that my brother had spent several years on an atoll in the Pacific as a navigator with the RNZAF.

One evening shortly before Christmas he surprised me by inviting me to a mess dinner at RAF Brize Norton. It was only then that I told him about Gordon's promise to me all those years ago. We must have looked an odd couple . . . an old lady with silver hair in a vintage 1950 little black dress and her stunning young escort in his elegant mess evening dress.

Gwen von Stemann

Beyond the Grave

the babysitter

'See how Richard is.'

'Yes, Mum,' again my response. Just six, head buried in a book. There were always books to read and comics galore. Mother sewing the endless repairs necessary for four boys and a builder. We always had babies around: Mother had a constant need for a baby to cherish. Babies, making a row, interrupting my reading.

'Go on then.'

'Yes, I'll just finish one page,' two, then three.

Sharply, 'You'll go now.'

I was well practiced; book down, run through the door from the kitchen into the hall, up the hall, around the newel and up to the landing. Two at a time, lightly, to avoid waking the baby, swing round the landing newel and the last two steps; into the bedroom in one smooth movement as usual.

Richard face down on the pillow, snuffling. That awful smell of baby vomit, how could Mum stand the constant pong? If it wasn't one end it was the other.

I'd seen her turn the babies so this was easy, except I couldn't get near the smell. Hands either side of his waist and arms straight I turned him to face me. Back to the book, run downstairs, shut the door and start at the open page.

'Is he all right?'

I didn't look up. 'Yes, Mum, his face was in the pillow but I've turned him round.'

I devoured the pages but it seemed only a few minutes before it was, 'Go and see Richard.'

'Yes, Mum.'

It took the usual 'Will you go now?' to budge me, into the hall, round the newel, up the stairs, swing round the last two steps, and – stop.

I slowly eased the door open, feet of lead as I walked in, turning slowly to look at the bed. Richard lay where I had found him before, face deep in the bolster pillow. As I knew when I'd reached the landing, he wasn't snuffling, not breathing at all. I looked at him, touched his stiff body, so still; of course, he was dead. Leaving him I walked down the stairs at the same leaden pace I had walked into the death room.

Slowly into the kitchen, quickly, 'What's the matter, is he all right?'

'Go and look at him, Mum,' in a small flat voice.

Voice rising, 'What's the matter?'

'Go and look at him, Mum,' the last still flat but

plaintive, as if she could understand only by seeing.

Mother's flight up the stairs was quicker than mine. It seemed she had only just run into the hall when that long anguished scream – 'No-o-o-o-o-o' – filled our ears. 'Oh, no, he can't be, he can't be.' Repeatedly, 'Oh no, no, no.'

Then I spoke: 'Richard's dead.'

Neighbours appeared; the ambulance arrived. All the while Mother trying to breath life into the small body, in vain of course: he had been too long without oxygen. The ambulance men must have told Mother quickly as her cries soon turned to helpless sobs. Father arrived to comfort her and after the inquest vowed, 'Never again, Nip.' He relented; eventually we were six lads and one girl.

Mother was questioned cruelly at the inquest. They implied she was guilty of killing him, she who gave everyone love so freely. I could have told them the truth. When I first turned Richard he was shaking and choking on vomit. As I left the room, I saw him turn again, but ignored it: my book beckoned and the vomit smelled awful. I'd been to see him, hadn't I?

Graham Wiggin

witness

When my son Gareth suggested I go with him and his wife Susan to South Wales for a long weekend I readily agreed. I was born in Llanelli and hadn't been back to visit my cousins for some time.

My cousins found us a place to stay. Susan had never been to Wales, so we visited some well-known beauty spots such as Tenby and St David's Head. Tired of sitting in the car, Susan said she felt like some exercise and we decided to drive into the countryside outside the town of Felinfoel, park the car, and do some walking. I was a bit dubious about being able to keep up with them as I was still recovering from a severe illness, but Gareth said we could stop and rest whenever I wanted to, so we set off.

After walking about two miles down country lanes I felt I really had to sit down. I told Gareth and Susan to continue and they could rejoin me on the way back. I found a grassy slope next to a stone wall, sat down and leaned back.

I must have dozed off in the warmth of the sun because I was woken by the sound of voices and in my sleepy state thought my son and his wife had returned. Luckily I didn't rise to my feet. A man and a woman, on the other side of the wall, were having an earnest discussion. The man said, 'We have to do something, we can't continue like this.' The woman replied that they had been through all this before and there was really only one solution. The man said, 'Yes, but she's very tough despite her age and poor health.'

The woman said, 'It's spring now and soon it will be too late to plant anything. She does love her blasted sheep. If I marry you she'll throw me out and leave the farm to Kevin. He'll probably rush back from Australia for her funeral.'

The pair went on to talk of ways of killing this poor woman and I listened, hardly able to believe my ears. Then they moved away and their voices faded. I stayed close to the wall, worried that Gareth and Susan would return and that we would all be noticed by the murderous couple. When my son and his wife returned about an hour later I told them what I had heard and Susan said I must go to the police and report them. But what would I be able to say? The people and the farm were unknown to me and we were leaving the next day.

Three months later I read in the newspaper that the

body of an elderly lady had been found bludgeoned to death on a farm near Felinfoel. The daughter's boyfriend had been arrested on suspicion of her murder.

Kathleen Gosden

On stony ground

'These stones will remain here forever. Forever! Wherever I cast them, there they will stay until Judgement Day. My Judgement Day. My stones. My family. They will be my memorial!'

Our cheeks reddened; Jacob's from his conviction; mine from the piercing wind in the country lane where, from a distance, I had seen him chucking stones into the hedgerows. I had noticed him before throwing his stones, often by a grove of towering beeches. I couldn't understand. This time I asked. The reply was an enigma. But so was Jacob. I was possibly his only friend; more of an acquaintance really. He had no family to my knowledge. Even so, he was liked in the village, shopping for pensioners and helping with the hospital car rota. But he kept himself to himself, his only group activity being his Saturday morning visit to the synagogue in the neighbouring town. Not far. So he walked – and threw the occasional stone. 'No harm,' he mused to himself. 'God will forgive me if I am breaking the Sabbath.'

'Your stones, Jacob?' I asked again. 'What is the meaning of your stones; why do you throw them anywhere and everywhere?'

The wind had become bitter. Wiping a growing droplet from his nose with the back of his hand Jacob paused before he replied: 'My friend, when I die there will be no one to visit my grave. There will be nobody to place a small stone on my gravestone as is customary in our religion. I have no family to say a prayer in my memory. So these stones that I now cast will be my memorial and they will remain here forever until I die and then they will return to me and be with me like the family I have never had.' With these words he smiled and turned. I watched his lean figure until it disappeared at the bend in the lane. I was puzzled. He had replied but not answered.

The months passed. Now and again I would see Jacob throwing his stones. Our paths crossed but rarely converged. Our conversation, when he decided to stop, was cursory. A token enquiry on health. A comment on the weather. No more.

I last saw Jacob on a late autumn day. The beeches had been slow to shed their leaves and they now glistened like burnished bronze in the glare of the low setting sun. Jacob stopped. His gauntness had become skeletal. A weak smile. That was all. No words passed between us; in a surprising gesture he just gripped my hand with a warmth that he had never shown before. I watched his lean figure disappear into the dying sun. I knew that he too was dying and that I would see him no more.

Jacob's synagogue had arranged his funeral and had set the gravestone one year later as was the convention. A note with my name had been found amongst his belongings. I was advised the location of his plot.

I first visited Jacob's grave some time after. A quantity of small stones were laid on it. I wondered by whom: he had not mentioned a family or close friends. For reasons I could not understand I was drawn to the cemetery to visit the grave more often. Each time the numbers of small stones had increased. There were now piles of them and they sparkled in the glow of a brilliant sun that always shone for my visits. I asked at the cemetery office. Nobody knew how the stones came to be placed on Jacob's grave. Whenever they were removed, inexplicably, they were replaced by more. But I knew. Jacob had scattered his stones; now, like the family he never had, they had returned to him as he said they would.

Paul Balen

through the spyhole

The doorknocker tapped hard: 'Please, let me in, I know you're in there.' I looked through the spyhole and saw a middle-aged, leather-coated woman with pinched features and dishevelled red hair, holding a bottle of wine. With a shake of her head, a slight totter and another 'I know you're in there', the woman turned and descended the four flights of cold steps that led down from my council flat in Shoreditch, east London. She came back after about twenty minutes and knocked loudly for five minutes. She did the same thing again some twenty minutes later.

Who was she? How could she be sure that I was in? I didn't open the door in the first place because I thought she would sober up soon enough and realise that she had the wrong door, the wrong person. I didn't open the door when she came back after that because by then I wanted to prove

266

a point – i.e., that there was no one at home. I had tied my own hands, as it were.

Still, during the third knocking I decided on action, for that time, with the wine bottle now half-empty, she used some foul, threatening language before chillingly leaving her verbal calling card: 'I know you're in there.' My phone was out of order, so I was going to ask someone to call the police. I opened my kitchen window at the back of the flat and looked down on to an afternoon street empty of life.

I returned to the living-room and sat once more at my rickety old desk. I was trying to write a lecture on an aspect of British politics. I'd just started teaching for the first time on a part-time basis at the Working Men's College, Camden Town. I had to complete it. I simply couldn't spare the time to engage with this woman. Perhaps I should have done, for the knocking began again.

Her thin, elegant hand with long fingers came through the letterbox and dropped two teabags 'as a peace-offering. I know you're in there . . .' I had a thought. I went into the living-room and looked out of the window at the adjacent block of flats. She must live directly opposite and could see me sitting at my desk! My curtains were open and there were no nets. But why was she so interested in me? Simple: she was drunk. I put my head out of the kitchen window and this time called to a middle-aged scruffy man walking his dog. 'Would you do me a favour? Could you please call the police. I live . . .'

'No,' he interjected in a gruff voice. He pulled the dog closer and made off down the road. The knocking stopped. Where were my neighbours?

I waited anxiously. The knocking started again. I didn't bother to look in the spyhole. I opened the door quickly and with mouth open stood rocking on my heels and facing a policeman.

'Has a woman been knocking on your door?'

I explained what had happened.

'Oh, that's a shame. If only you had opened the door to her once. You see, she had a terrible argument with her partner. They live together on this estate. She got plastered and went back to try and make it up.'

'But why my door?'

'Twenty-nine: same door number, but she got the wrong building. It's the next building.'

After the woman had knocked for the third time she threw herself off my front-door balcony. I finished my lecture. She died.

Leonard Stone

Gangster boogie

Decades ago, as a humble and somewhat seedy pen-pusher in the great big City of London, it was my wont to haunt low pubs in the murkier purlieus of Stepney. I was a lone voyeur seeking, with modest half pints, something of interest or wonder in the lower depths. It was Jack the Ripper territory.

The night was young in an almost-empty bar when I was enjoined by some ladies of the night to dance with them to some old piano tunes. Past their prime, they habitually enjoyed glasses of Guinness before plying their nocturnal trade.

They much appreciated the skill with which I steered their buxom bodies around the holes in the dusty brown lino, and I was rewarded with some raucous cheers. It was this that brought me to the attention of a young girl who, unlike the night-ladies, was fresh, slim and, without question, beautiful.

'Dance with me,' this nymphet demanded. Her face was flushed and had an unusual expression, and her outstretched arms were insistent.

I was more than flattered. Back in the office the chaps might regard me as a back number. They should see me now with this stunning girl who fancied me. And she was half my age.

She was in the company of three men in smart new suits with well-padded shoulders. When they pushed the girl a liqueur, they didn't give her a glance. Engrossed in conversation, their backs appeared forbidding, which made me pause in some doubt.

Nevertheless, when the jangling piano struck a lively tune, I danced with the girl.

Well, not precisely 'with'. She was whirling like a dervish, twisting and turning with more violence than grace, pushing and pulling so that the fragrance of her hair in my face made me dizzy. I forced her to stand still.

'Look, sweetie,' I said quietly. 'You are wonderful, but we can't dance if you don't behave.'

'No,' she pleaded. 'Don't stop. I've been locked in a room for four days. I must dance.' This fair maiden is on drugs, I surmised, but I humoured her.

'Which one is your partner?' I asked.

'The one on the end,' she said, and I approached him.

'Excuse me,' I said respectfully to his broad back. 'The young lady wants to dance – is that all right?'

'Yes,' said the gruff voice. 'But watch it.'

Yet the dancing girl was uncontrollable. Her twists and

turns made our bodies collide, which was very pleasant, but over her shoulder I could see the three tough men. They didn't seem interested, but I felt it was time for discretion. Stepping back I turned quickly on my heel and disappeared into the Stepney night.

A week later I entered the bar again. 'Gordon Bennett!' cried the barmaid. 'He's still alive.'

'Of course,' I puzzled. 'Why not?'

'Blimey,' she said. 'That girl you was taking liberties with – blokes have lost their ears for less than that.'

'I took no liberties,' I protested. 'It was her.'

'Don't matter,' she shrugged. 'That was Reggie Kray's wife. You were lucky.'

Later, after my escape, l learnt that my dancing girl committed suicide and the brothers were jailed for murder and mayhem. I found better things to do, but will never forget the girl who needed to dance so much.

Peter Perry

A picture of grief

I was nineteen years old. I had gone to France with a friend of a friend to train as a photographer. It was 1950. I knew very little French – less than I knew about photography. But I was working for a talented commercial photographer who was going to teach me a whole world of technical skills. I was lucky, but I had never worked so hard, and I had to get used to the French way of life, the food, the inevitable upset stomach, and the loneliness that resulted from my poor grasp of the language.

Before I was allowed out with a camera on my own I went about with the *patron*, my boss, working as his assistant, handing him his lenses, a tripod, cameras I had primed with fresh rolls of film, and so on.

One hot sunny day we drove to a village in Loiret. During the journey my boss tried hard to explain something to me. He seemed absolutely determined, but what he said made no real sense to me. Eventually, he shrugged his shoulders and gave up. We arrived at the village, parked the car and removed the box of equipment we were going to use. I felt happy with myself, the weather, and my decision to come here and learn professional photography.

We walked to our destination from the car-park. I remember I was whistling softly. As we walked I suddenly had an ominous feeling that something was wrong, something tragic. I stopped whistling, and we entered a little house. We immediately found ourselves in a small, dingy room. There, lying on a settee, was a pretty young woman, very pale and tearful, looking for all the world as if her death was just around the corner. With her was a young man who I took to be her husband, and two older people who I took to be parents. They were all tearful.

They spoke quickly and sadly, and I wondered what on earth we were doing there. Perhaps to photograph the dying girl? After a little more talk, they all stood up and opened a door that I had not noticed, revealing a flight of stairs. We followed them up and went into a room that had the blinds drawn.

The blinds were opened. The sun sent shafts of light through the small windows, and there in a cot, lying as if in sleep, was a newborn baby – dead. For the first and only time in my life, my legs felt like jelly, and I nearly fell. I held on to a piece of furniture. This was why we were here. We had to photograph this poor little child before it was put in its coffin and buried. Here was the sadness and grief. In a daze I handed my boss the gear: a tripod, some lights, the camera. The shots were taken.

I couldn't have been more pleased to get out of that house and into the fresh air once again. But I soon had to blot out my memory of that particular job, at least in the short term, as we went off to photograph a wedding.

Harold Morris

killing time

It was Monday. Johnno, Barry, Alan, Tony, Smithy, Ian and I glanced expectantly at the clock, willing the hands to move round to 3.30 p.m. At nine years of age a whole summer's day in school was torture. At last the minute-hand clicked round to six, and that meant freedom was imminent. The bell monitor had started on the bottom floor so the infants could leave the building first, and he was now walking slowly along the top corridor, clanging the brass handbell as hard as he could. The teacher stood and said, 'All books away. Line up by the door.' There was no need for any other instruction, as the class had done this many times before. Girls first, followed by the boys. We were escorted to the top of the stairs by Mr Walton and sent home. Progress down the stairs was slowed by the 11-year-old prefects, whose favourite trick was to push you down the stairs then

275

hit you for running. After what seemed an age we entered the playground, and our gang collected by the large iron gates. We talked excitedly, for the twentieth time that day, about how good the main film had been at the Saturday morning pictures. It had been a Lone Ranger special in which the Masked Avenger and his faithful companion Tonto had defeated the Apaches, who were trying to kill the soldiers in the fort.

We divided into two groups and ran off down the road, with the Apaches chasing the cowboys. The bombsite at the corner of the road by the off-licence doubled as the High Plains, and before long the cowboys had killed all the Apaches. With no one left to kill or wound, we strolled down the street, to where we lived.

It was Johnno who first saw the ambulance and police car outside number six. We stopped outside the house and watched. There was a terrible smell of gas, and I heard the policeman say to the ambulance man that she had gassed herself. There was also a note. None of us boys knew what it all meant. Mrs Clarke was brought out on a stretcher. She was very still, her eyes closed and her face a colour I could not describe. Her arms hung limply off the stretcher. Mr Clarke walked behind, and it looked as if he had been crying. 'What's happened?' Ian asked.

The policeman chased us away. We walked cautiously past number six and then I broke into a gallop, running towards the bakers with the outlaws, Johnno, Barry and Alan, pursued by Tony, Smithy and Ian, who were the sheriff and his posse. By the time we reached the bakers all the sheriff's men were either badly wounded or dead.

Once we reached the bakers we had grown bored with killing each other and so we played football. By the time the ambulance containing Mr and Mrs Clarke went by, West Ham were easily beating Fulham.

My grandmother called me in for my tea. I left the game and walked through the gate that led to the prefab. Nan was talking to my grandfather.

'It is a real shame. They seemed such a happy couple. He came home from work and found her on the kitchen floor. The policeman said she had probably been dead since early this morning.' She gave me my favourite tea, which was a bacon and tomato sandwich. I ate as I read the *Eagle* comic, devouring the pages where the Mekon was trying to blast Dan Dare and his spaceship out of the sky.

Gerry Denton

Final reminder

My father died of Alzheimer's disease. I was an only child – his treasure, or 'treash' for short – and I was much loved. I always say my father died several years before his physical death. That bald statement hides years of travail and misery. For the last two years he didn't recognise me, and lived incarcerated in care homes. He escaped twice, once getting all the way from Edinburgh to Glasgow while heavily sedated, with no money and only a letter from me in his pocket to identify him. He ended up in the arms of a British Transport Police sergeant, who was sympathetic and telephoned me to collect him. I kept my father for one night and found another place for him.

The real problem was that his dementia made him violent and aggressive. As a result, he drove away all those who tried to help. My mother was a nervous wreck, despite having 24-hour nursing care and locked rooms to keep him in. Eventually he was admitted to a special unit for confused and elderly patients, which had just opened in Blackburn. There were security doors and large, white-T-shirted bruisers to make sure no one escaped. There were only twelve patients in the unit, both men and women. They all had individual foibles. One woman had been a telephonist, and they gave her a toy telephone to answer hundreds of times a day. Another, who had been a seamstress, picked up imaginary threads, rolled them in her hands into non-existent balls which she put into an invisible ashtray. A man who had been a soldier used to shout 'Attention!' several times a day; he scared sane people, but the other inmates ignored him. My father used to get up from his seat, do a little jig, and sit down again. I never found out why.

After about four months at Blackburn, the fight went out of him. He had what I used to describe as 'dive-downs', when, after a period of stability, he would suddenly get worse, and have even less recall afterwards. One day he had a particularly bad dive-down after which he seemed to shrink. By this time he had virtually no memory of anything. We were able to get him into a small home near my mother, where the staff could monitor him on CCTV. He was virtually catatonic, not knowing those around him, nor his family. We had kept his grandchildren away for over two years.

One day when I went to visit him, the staff nurse asked me if I could try to cut his fingernails. 'He won't let anyone touch his hands,' she said. 'It's very strange.' She gave me a pair of nail scissors and I went into his room.

He was sitting on the bed staring at the wall, shrunken, spectral. I greeted him as I always had: 'Hello, Dad.' He stared at me blankly. I burbled on about nothing and then said, 'Is that the length of your nails? Is no one looking after you?' I took his hand and showed it to him. He looked at it, deadpan. I took the scissors and quickly cut the nails on one hand, then the other. 'There. That's much better.' I stayed for another half hour, sitting on the bed beside him, speaking of this and that, none of which elicited any response. Before I rose to go, I gave him a hug, and said, 'Bye, Dad.'

As I stood up, he lay back on the bed, turning away from me. 'Bye bye, Treash, God bless.' The next time I saw him he was in his coffin.

Douglas Mitchell

A line in the sand

My father was the youngest in a family of ten children, and he was considered a bit of a nuisance – not only because he was, but because *his* father had died shortly before his birth, leaving the family strapped for cash.

My grandmother managed to get all the children a good education by the energetic writing of begging letters. Gladys, the second eldest, became a physiotherapist and, unlike some of her other sisters (there were seven girls and three boys), she was kind to little Tony, my father. She read him stories when she wasn't at college, and helped him learn to swim. (All the children apart from Tony – who was spared the ordeal by his father's death – had been taught to swim by the dubious method of throwing them into the local swimming-pool and encouraging them to make it to the side.) Gladys was old enough to have been my father's mother, and remained especially close to him all her life. She always remembered his birthday, 5 November, and when Gladys was a very old lady, a tiny little figure not even 5ft tall, she said to my father, 'Tony, wherever I am, wherever you are, I shall always remember you on your birthday!'

Shortly after, she died at the age of ninety. My father, being the youngest, found it a terrible burden to see his siblings die one by one before him. He did not voice these sentiments to me, but my mother told me how he felt. So, on his birthday, following Gladys's death, I went to see my parents at their house on the south coast. After a good lunch we faced the gloom of late autumn, pulled on our boots and jackets and set off along the beach. It started off with some scrubby plants, sea holly and sea spinach (delicious with scrambled egg on toast), before turning into piles of shingle – difficult to walk on. As the tide receded, sand was revealed with puddles of water. The beach is controlled by a legion of breakwaters, punctuating the coastline and creating a kind of hurdling challenge for walkers. Across the Solent, a slash of pewter-coloured water below a dark lilac sky, the lights were beginning to come on in Cowes, and we wondered how far we would be able to walk before turning back for a cup of tea and a slice of birthday cake.

We trudged along, not exactly enjoying the walk but feeling that it was good for us to get out. Conversation didn't flow. I asked my mother about her Italian class in nearby Chichester, plans for Christmas and family news. My father was walking ahead of us, thinking his own thoughts, a burly figure against the fading light.

'Let's turn back,' he shouted, his woolly hat now firmly pulled down over his ears. 'I'm getting cold . . . and it'll soon be dark.' He sounded at that moment like a small boy again.

We turned our backs against a watery sunset, and headed eastwards along the beach. We counted the number of breakwaters we had yet to climb over until we would reach the garden gate, and remarked on the fact that we had hardly seen a soul all afternoon. Clambering over the last breakwater into the final stretch we stopped, all three of us. For there before us, gleaming in the wet sand, written in huge letters by an unknown hand, was the one word: GLADYS.

Molly Verity

Many years ago my mother had a dear friend who was interested in spiritualism and regularly held séances at her home. My mother was very sceptical and always refused her friend's invitations to join the group. However, after my mother received yet another invitation, my aunt suggested that she really should attend a meeting, and then come back and tell the family about all her experiences.

Although unwilling to go – partly for fear she should giggle, and partly because she was uneasy about the whole thing – she agreed to attend, just for the one time.

So it was, on the evening in question, that she turned up and took her place among the dozen or so people in the meeting-room. Lights were turned low and the meeting began with a visiting medium telling her audience that she was in contact with the spirit of a young Glaswegian boy who had been killed in a road crash. My mother was more sceptical than ever, but sat quietly. In a short time the medium fell silent, then began to speak in a broad Glaswegian accent, the voice telling the meeting that 'he' was Bobbie. He told the gathering of his accident and that he was there to help the living to get in touch with their dear departed friends and relatives, if it was possible. Several people asked questions and were answered – whether genuinely or not, my mother couldn't tell, as she had never met them before.

Suddenly the voice changed and became louder. Bobbie laughed as he spoke his next words. 'Jenny Gibson is here tonight! It's y'r first time here, isn't it?'

My mother, more than a little shaken, was hardly able to speak, but she mumbled 'Yes'.

Worse was to come. Bobbie continued, 'Aye, Ah can see y'. Ah've been having a wee game wi' y'. Y'lost a funny steel thing wi' a hook on the end about two weeks ago, didn'y'?'

Mum again mumbled a 'Yes', then added, 'You mean my crochet hook?'

'Ay! Ah hid it.' My mother remained silent, so Bobbie continued: 'D'y' no' want to know what ah did wi' it?'

'Yes, please, I need it.'

'Y'know thon settee y'huv that comes doon inta a bed?'

'Yes.'

'Weel! Y've looked and looked but y've no found it, huv y'? Weel, Ah pit it in yon settee-bed that y've been using a' this last week. Y'go and look again when y'get back home an' y'll see.'

Mum sat silent for the rest of the meeting, torn between

believing the boy's words and thinking what nonsense it was. She would have dismissed the whole thing utterly but was puzzled as to how he could possibly know about the fold-down sofa, or that she was indeed currently using it for me to sleep in. She arrived home very shaken and told my aunt the story.

My aunt was unbelieving. 'Jenny, that's rubbish, it's coincidence or guessing. Let's go and search the bed. It won't be there, we have shaken that mattress each morning for a week.'

But it was. Sitting right in the centre of the mattress as the boy had said it would be.

My mother never again mocked spiritualism. Nor did she ever attend another séance.

June Raper

286

Dead cert

My father-in-law was a big, florid-faced man of Irish descent. He liked his beer, his horses and his own way. He was not an easy man to like and by the time I came to know him he was well established in both his career and his opinions. Family and friends had learnt to acquiesce around him and he was therefore far from pleased to have a young woman take up his family name who was not also prepared to accept his every opinion.

My husband and I lived and worked some distance from our parents' homes so a visit to them always involved a weekend stay. At the house of my husband's parents Saturdays were taken up with my father-in-law watching the horse-racing on television in the sitting-room, jumping up every now and then to place a bet over the telephone. That I would never join in this activity really irked him and he was always at pains to tell me how sound were his judgements and how financially successful the outcome.

Because the sitting-room was combined with the dining area into one large space, the rest of the family was confined to the kitchen. Our only other option was to abandon the house altogether and take a walk or a trip into town to wander aimlessly around the shops and covered market. Sunday lunches waited for his imminent, but always delayed, return from the pub. It was all very far from my idea of a happy family weekend and long, uncomfortable years lay ahead of us.

Eventually my father-in-law came to realise that my opinions would remain my own, one of them being that I thought betting on the horses was a mug's game. He had an opinion on everything and no subject was safe; politics and education were to be avoided at all cost. Once sufficiently goaded, I found it hard not to respond, in spite of the frantic, silent messages from my husband involving frowns, raised eyebrows and dramatically rolling eyes, all done behind his father's back. His father reached a solution by holding forth on a favourite topic and then, nodding in my direction, he would say, 'Well, we know what you think!' Having dispensed with me without my needing to open my mouth, he could then continue his soliloquy.

He was a powerfully built man who loved his food but, gradually, as his weight increased his health deteriorated. The damage done, the weight then started to fall away from him and as his illness developed he became un-characteristically subdued and passive. My husband made several journeys to his parents' home but I did not see my father-in-law again. Not long after my husband had visited him in hospital, we received a phone call saying that his father had died. Before the funeral my brother-in-law had a message to pass on to us from his father. We had to place a bet on a horse that he knew would win on Derby Day. My brother-in-law had already done as his father had told him. We, as usual, declined.

I was surprised with what ease the coffin was carried down the centre aisle of the chapel, unable to think of my father-in-law as anything other than large and powerful. It was Derby Day and his horse was running as the funeral took place. The odds were sixteen to one. It turned out to be a winner and its name was Dr Devious.

Isabella McIllroy

Graveyard shift

My daughter went to a disco in our local church hall. 'No need for you to pick me up, I'll be getting a lift home with my friend,' she said, and I looked forward to a quiet evening in.

An early bath was luxurious, after which I put on a comfortable white towelling dressing-gown and curled up with the latest library book, pleasurably thinking of an early night. I was already in bed when the telephone rang at 11.30 p.m. My daughter's lift home had failed to materialise, so could she be picked up? My heart sank; it would mean a half-mile drive to the church when I was by now warm and cosy in bed. The last thing I felt like doing was dressing and going out.

But then – a brilliant idea! Why bother to put clothes on? Why not go in my dressing-gown? The evening wasn't particularly cold. Besides, it was late and dark, and the church was in an unpopulated area, so who, apart from the teenagers, would be likely to be there at midnight? And in any case I would be in the car, so no one would see me.

The church was situated out of the village, and driving along the quiet country lane, lit only by a weak moon, I congratulated myself on the decision not to get changed. I had been proved right: not a soul was around, not even another car to intrude on the stillness. The only living creature was a fox whose bright eyes shone in the car's headlights before it beat a hasty retreat into the undergrowth.

I parked in a secluded lane behind the church, from where I could take a diagonal short cut across the churchyard to the hall. Hitching up my dressing-gown I made my way in the direction of the light, picking a passage between dimly visible tombstones. As I was halfway along the route voices from a nearby path floated towards me. 'Ah, that will be my daughter and her friends,' I thought, and turned to locate them.

It was a terrible mistake. The next moment I was sprawled flat on my face across a mounded grave, thrown off balance by a tombstone protruding unnoticed from the ground.

That's when the moon emerged from behind the clouds, illuminating the area as I stumbled to my feet – a figure in white, silhouetted against a tombstone. Abruptly, the laughing chatter stopped. A second of deathly silence hung on the air before giving way to a series of ear-splitting shrieks that would have aroused the banshee. Immediately, the pounding of half a dozen teenage feet, frantically struggling to reach the safety of the church hall, could be heard on the pathway.

I waved, I called, all to no avail; panic had set in and no one intended to stop and face a dangerous unknown. For a minute or two I waited, concealed beneath the protective branches of an overhanging yew tree. It seemed the prudent thing to do. Then I crept forward, negotiating a way towards the footpath and the church hall.

In a shaft of light from the hall stood a bewildered vicar surrounded by a bunch of gibbering, gabbling teenagers. As he looked up, the situation began to dawn on him. At the same time several pairs of accusatory teenage eyes fixed me with a steady, reproachful gaze.

We walked to the car in silence – my daughter and the two friends who wanted a lift. My daughter spoke first. 'You should have worn a coat. No one else would come out in a dressing-gown.' But support was forthcoming. The youngest, an eleven-year-old, piped up, '*My* mummy might have done.' My self-esteem was restored.

Patricia Peters

Suicide watch

I spend a lot of time looking out of my kitchen window. I can see the lawns and beds of our garden, which slopes down to a broad, mudflatted estuary. And I've got a brilliant view of the high road-bridge over the river that opened a few years ago.

My husband and I keep two sets of binoculars on the windowsill. Most people assume they're for watching the gulls and other marine birds that flock along the mudflats, or even for spying on the neighbours. But they're actually for looking at the bridge. More specifically, they're for looking at people jumping off the bridge.

Since the bridge opened about fifteen years ago, it's become a favoured spot for suicides. Scores of people have jumped or attempted to jump. There's a walkway across it, and the barriers are pretty low. They have a banner in the middle now, with a Samaritans helpline number on it, but it doesn't seem to deter people. We saw the first one even before the bridge was completed. A woman. I was actually looking out for herons at the time; our goldfish pond was being decimated. I thought it was strange that she was up there; it was a Sunday, and I assumed she must be taking a walk or something. But then she scrambled over the parapet and went straight in. No hesitation. I watched her all the way down. It happened very fast. She hit the water – the tide was in – and went under. Someone must have called the lifeboat, because it turned up a few minutes later and fished her out. I had a stiff drink and told my husband what I'd seen. He said he was sorry he'd missed it. He was kind of joking, but we bought his set of binoculars soon afterwards.

I know it sounds callous, but we've seen so many of them now, it's almost like some kind of bizarre reality TV show happening through our window. People behave very differently once they get themselves up there. Some walk up and down for hours and just drift off again. Some stand looking out, screwing up their courage, I suppose, before clambering over and looking around, maybe hoping someone will come along and persuade them out of it. Sometimes cars slow down and drivers try to talk them down. Some fling their arms out when they jump, like Jesus. Some just sort of slip off, like they want to go quietly. But you wouldn't believe how quickly they fall once they're airborne. You can't afford to blink.

It's almost like we've become amateur experts in suicide lore. We've seen more women than men make attempts, though men are more 'successful'; most people pick the spot where the bridge's span is highest, although that means they're more likely to land in the water, even when the tide's out (we've never seen anyone plummet into the mud, though my husband swore he'd once seen someone hit one of the concrete bridge supports as they landed, which shook him up a bit); the jump-rate seems to be higher if the police are on the scene.

My family take me to task on this. 'You do call the police, of course?' they ask. I mean, of course we do if they've actually gone in the water and there's no one else around. But the police usually turn up eventually, in any case.

'Why don't you go the whole hog?' they ask. 'Invite people round for tea and biscuits, get them to bring their own binoculars, have a little suicide party?'

Mary Broad

christmas

Fowl mood

'Delivered on the 23rd? Fine. Thank you very much.' Before
I put down the phone I added as an afterthought, 'Dressed
of course.' A plump oven-ready turkey, the giblets cleaned
and wrapped in plastic. The countdown to Christmas was
going well. It hadn't always been so. The years fell away and
I remembered one of our first Christmases abroad. My
husband's work took us to Africa a few short years after we
were married, a thrilling experience for two young people
but, with two babies in tow, also a tremendous upheaval in
our so-far placid lives.

There were other British families working out there and
we soon made friends with another newly arrived couple.
We were wondering how we could simulate a traditional
Christmas without the mandatory holly and snow, log fires
and a Christmas tree. A colleague said he knew a farm that

sold chickens but it was ninety miles away. We phoned our order and arranged to collect. 'We' were two young married women, one heavily pregnant, and me with our two toddlers. We had become used to long journeys across boiling hot, barren land – and the difficulty of keeping the children amused throughout. Besides, the thought of roast chicken on the dinner table spurred us on.

We arrived hot and dusty. The farmer's wife was a large-framed white South African, with skin weathered by sun and wind. 'Pick your own.' She gestured to a compound where several hundred hens were pecking in the dirt. 'This one, and this one, and how about this one?' she offered. Horrified we watched as she placed them in a sack. Panic rose in my throat. Alison began to giggle hysterically.

'Aren't you going to kill them?' I ventured, as the truth began to dawn.

'You didn't ask for them dressed,' she replied firmly, securing a knot in the sack and handing over the squawking birds. Alison had gone quite pale and I was feeling sick as I marched back to the car holding the sack at arm's length.

The return trip was a nightmare. From the back of the car six heads protruded from the sack, occasionally making convulsive sounds. Six pairs of eyes stared resentfully at the backs of our heads. Twice we had to stop while Alison was sick. The children, at least, were quiet, intimidated by the new passengers breathing down their necks.

'What's this, then?' Don cried as I lifted the now smelly sack from the car.

'This,' I said triumphantly, 'is your Christmas dinner. We did the collecting, now it's your turn!'

'Not likely,' he cried, hurrying away.

Alison's husband confidently announced that he knew what to do. 'You just pull their necks and twist . . . like this', and he demonstrated this simple method in mid air. Relieved we willingly passed on the task to him.

In the event it proved more difficult than he had supposed. He confessed he had never actually wrung a chicken's neck but that it had looked straightforward when he had seen it done. I shudder now as I recall the terrible inexpert ways we tried to kill those unfortunate birds.

We ate the chickens. In fact we enjoyed our Christmas. But never again did I order poultry without stressing that it must be 'dressed' for the table.

Marjorie Wynn

Keeping up with the Joneses

We used to live in a cul-de-sac of twenty houses and, although it was in a large town, residents of The Close prided themselves on its village atmosphere. It was a friendly street – children played in each other's houses and at Christmas all the neighbours ate mince pies and drank mulled wine together. Of course there were downsides too; we all knew a bit too much about one another.

Houses in The Close rarely changed hands, so when a great friend moved to another town she promised to vet the buyers to make sure our new neighbours would be really nice and would 'fit in'. But in the end she didn't have the time; she had to move in a hurry, and the first we saw of our new neighbours were the teams of workmen. There were marble-floor layers, posh-kitchen fitters and a firm of very grand interior decorators whose vans blocked the street for

302

weeks on end. The local handyman who slapped a few coats of Farrow & Ball on most of the other houses was plainly not getting a look in at number eleven.

Bill and Kiko Jones moved in just before Christmas. He was huge, tanned and shaven-headed, with one enormous diamond earring; she small, silent and Japanese. At the Christmas drinks parties he was loud and jovial with a ferocious cockney accent; she said not a word. We learnt that they had not been married long and that he had just sold his dry-cleaning business in the East End – and while we all longed to know more about them, they evaded our implied questions.

When the Joneses turned up on our doorstep on Christmas Eve bearing a lavish present for each of our children (including the PlayStation we had promised our son if he got into his new school), my husband was furious. 'But they are only trying to be *nice*,' I said, after they had left.

'Huh!' he replied. 'Give him a stripey jumper and bag marked swag. Dry-cleaning indeed! Getaway driver for a gang of bank robbers, more like.'

We didn't see much more of the Joneses after that – he didn't seem to go out to work and she, having no children, did not join the morning tramp to the local primary school.

Although we were mainly young families in The Close, our next-door neighbour was a frail, elderly widow, Mrs Priest. She lived with her son, Peter, who sang semi-professionally in church choirs. During the summer holidays, while he was away with his singing group, Mrs Priest locked herself out of the house. She was very distressed. 'I have to get in to take my midday pill,' she kept saying in a quavering voice.

Most of the street was away on holiday – we had stayed at home as I was expecting a baby any day. I rang several locksmiths but could not find anyone willing to come quickly. Mrs Priest (who was almost in tears), the children and I were standing looking at the house with its high drawing-room windowsill and firmly locked basement door and window, when Bill Jones walked up. On hearing our problem he seemed to hesitate for a few moments. Then, launching himself on to the sill, he swiftly opened the locked window, dived into the house and appeared grinning at the front seconds later: ''Ere we are, then.'

'Good Lord!' said Mrs Priest as she thanked him and slowly walked up the steps. 'Where did you learn to do that?'

Bill Jones's face turned scarlet under his perma-tan as he and I stared at each other.

Margaret Wadsworth

What goes up

I can still recall the magic of believing in Father Christmas. I remember the dark Christmas sky, the pine-sweet smell as we crouched under the Christmas tree 'hiding' while it was decorated. Then lo and behold! The dazzling spots of glass were switched on above us, all the baubles reflecting their light and bouncing it around the room. Fairyland!

That Christmas Eve began much like any other. We hadn't been able to persuade Dad to put a ladder up to hoist a blow-up Father Christmas at the top of the house like the Turners opposite, but nevertheless we went to bed excited, confident that Father Christmas would brave the chimney as he always did. Bedtime was when the real Christmas fun began. Wrapped in woolly patchwork, my sister Jane and I knelt side by side on the dressing table under the window, like two Russian dolls, with a store of saved up sweets close to hand to see us through the 'Christmas watch'. Everyone did the watch. Jamie three doors down claimed he did it with his father's binoculars, but Carl, his older brother, gave him a look of disdain and disbelief (Carl did decimals so we believed him).

The Turners were having a grown-up party. We could see through their new patio doors groups of chattering people clasping glasses of drink – 'booze', Carl called it. Our parents had gone there briefly but returned because Mum wanted to make mince pies and put sherry out for Father Christmas. It was not quite their scene, they said. By about ten o'clock we could tell that the party was dragging. People were becoming quieter and flopping on to sofas, and by about 10.30 most of the cars had left. Only a few stragglers remained, smoking in the front garden. We wished they'd leave, too: we were worried they would frighten the reindeer off. No one seemed to notice the man in the red anorak start to climb the ladder. It was difficult to see clearly but he seemed to have something – could it be a sack? – over his shoulder, and a bottle under his other arm. His progress was slow, one unsteady foot following the other like Grandpa going up the stairs. Once he had reached the fourth or fifth rung, people started to notice, and to giggle nervously, and one man rushed forward to steady the ladder. I thought I heard Mrs Turner call out, 'Come down Steven, you fool!'

Father Christmas had almost reached halfway when he did a strange thing. With his stomach resting against the ladder for balance, he let go. Then, flinging out his sack arm, he raised the bottle high with the other, and shouted to the smokers below, 'Long live Father Christmas!' The sack flew from his grasp, hit a nearby drainpipe and slithered silently down to the ground, to land with a thump at the same moment he did. We were aghast. We jumped back to bed – we didn't want to see any more; we didn't want to know! There was a bit of a hubbub over the road but we dived under the icy bedclothes to escape it all. Jane's muffled voice said there was no need to worry – Father Christmas was magic, wasn't he? He was unbreakable. He couldn't ever die!

It was very quiet across the road for over a week. Then an ambulance drew up outside the Turners, its two back doors were opened, and Mr Turner was carefully lowered out in a wheelchair. He was wearing his red anorak and both his legs were in plaster.

Christmas has never been quite as magical since.

Jennifer Percival

Guess who's coming to dinner?

Whenever I tell people that one year we had a tramp for Christmas, I am guaranteed one of two answers. I am asked for the recipe, or I am advised that my listener usually has a turkey. Either response is accompanied by loud guffaws as if it were the first time I'd heard it.

I first met Brian on a December morning when I arrived early at church to fill the urn and set out the biscuits for after the service. I have never minded being there by myself but that morning I shivered with the sense that I was not alone. Peering round in the gloom I saw the familiar chairs and pulpit, and gave myself a shake, knowing that I had only just unlocked the door so there could be no one else in the building. But still, the feeling persisted; I kept glancing at my watch hoping the congregation would arrive. Then I heard the sobbing. Making my way back into the church from the vestry, I saw a large figure in a dark overcoat, hunched in the front row, shaking in spasms of grief. I gave him some of the tea I'd prepared, and quietly listened as he sobbed out his sad tale. He had once had a good job, a home and a close-knit family, but had lost it all. Now he slept under an upturned boat on the beach and sat in an abandoned car during the day, writing poetry. He was clearly troubled and kept looking round, saying 'they' were following him. I should have felt threatened being alone in the church with a disturbed stranger, but I didn't. When I asked where he'd be on Christmas Day, he shrugged and replied, 'On the beach as usual.'

I swear that I said nothing but I heard my voice answer, 'Not this year. You are coming home with me.' Telling my husband was easy, as his family has always kept 'open Christmas', putting up trestle tables to feed anyone who would otherwise be alone. His only worry was that Brian might be reluctant to go back to his upturned boat after the comfort of our centrally heated home. My vicar expressed fears that we could be opening our home to a possible axe-murderer, but I went ahead with my plans, buying socks and gloves for our extra guest to unwrap. My own fears were that our grandsons were at an age when they would giggle uncontrollably for no reason. Would Brian's long withdrawal from polite society provide the trigger to set them off? I called a family conference and laid down some rules. No matter what Brian did, or how his manners might let him down, he was a guest in our house and must be treated with respect.

In the event, our fears were groundless and it was a

lovely day. Somehow Brian's presence in the house put everyone on their best behaviour and there was no squabbling. As soon as he arrived, still looking over his shoulder for 'them', he asked if he could wash and shave. After a long soak in the bath, he came down looking smarter and younger, smelling of everything our bathroom had to offer. Before leaving, he asked how much he owed us, then asked if he might read a poem. Thinking it would be one he had written in his car, we sat expectantly as he unfolded a grubby piece of paper and began to recite the words of 'Eleanor Rigby' about lonely people, where they come from, and where they belong. I only saw Brian once after that. He was in a doorway, sharing a bottle of milk with an old dog he held on a hairy string. As I drove past, I felt glad that he now had a friend to share his cold nights on the beach, and I wondered if he was still writing his poetry.

Mary Mann

Home and dry

Summer was scarcely over in 1954 before my mother was busy making the Christmas pudding. Winter comes early on the Baltic coast where we were living, the only British family in town. Indoors, my family maintained the English tradition of stirring the pudding mixture and making a wish. 'A wish will only come true if you don't tell it,' we were warned. 'Keep it a secret and you'll have your wish by Christmas.' I wished and wished as I stirred and kept my mouth shut tight as I helped poke in the silver threepenny bits, saved from one pudding to the next (unless inadvertently swallowed).

Days shortened and the earth froze. Early December brought the Feast of Saint Nicholas, when children's slippers were stuffed with gifts. On that day, for me, came a gleam of hope. At short notice my father was directed back to Britain. The household was suddenly in upheaval. Rooms were awash with newspaper as china was wrapped and stuffed into packing-cases. No occasion this year for a candle-decked wreath or *Adventskranz*, though we did find room in a trunk for the Christmas pudding, and a bottle of rum. In Hamburg, where we stopped en route to the Hook of Holland, festoons of lights danced to their reflections in the waters of the River Alster – a fairyland for a child who didn't notice the bombsites and jagged ruins. In contrast, when we reached the Hook, the North Sea coast held no magic. Within minutes of being on the quayside we were a forlorn, rain-drenched family, gripping hands and baggage, and all the more forlorn when separated from my father. This was a troop ship, the sexes firmly segregated. Women and children were stowed deep below decks where the children clamoured, whined and wailed.

Trying to be sensible and good, I obediently undressed and settled on a top bunk, more roused than lulled by the throbbing engines and the sea's swell. Fairly soon, the bedlam within the cabin was subsumed in the madness of the elements. Teddy bears, feeding bottles, dummies, children and vomit flew from the bunks. In the passage outside, the steward's china-cupboard burst open, flinging out broken crockery to splinter under the feet of anyone out there still able to stand. By midnight, when (we later learnt) the ship was actually being blown backwards, bruising, injuries and broken limbs had compounded the misery of the majority already prostrated by sea-sickness.

Throughout the storm I wasn't sick, calming myself with my secret mantra: 'I wish . . .', hoping against hope, as the ferry, eight hours late, nosed into Harwich on the morning of Christmas Eve.

Ambulances awaited the storm-wounded; we limped down the gangway and were reunited with my father who, scarcely recognisable with his black eye, was clutching a Fry's chocolate bar – the only food to come our way all night. Then, at Liverpool Street, as the station clock touched noon, we breakfasted on fish and chips wrapped in a London newspaper. The Cornish Riviera Express, steaming west through a sodden storm-wracked landscape, was luxury. The waiter brought us English toasted tea-cakes with English jam; there was gently murmured polite conversation. In the fast-fading light I saw Hereford cattle and Southdown sheep in tidy English hedged-fields. Names of English towns and villages flashed by. Passing Southampton, we glimpsed the *Queen Mary*.

It was after nightfall, past bedtime, when we tumbled out at the little Dorset station. Herbert was on the platform, with a wheelbarrow for our luggage. As we rounded the lane I could see, through the Bramley apple-tree boughs, the porch light shining, the door open. I had made it: home to England for Christmas, with three hours to spare.

Helen Gichard

Heat and dust

I was born on a farm in southern Africa where my life was coloured by the wide open spaces and the enormous skies of the African bush. When I grew up I married a geologist and many nights were spent sitting around a camp fire and gazing into the vastness of the sky, where the stars stretched to infinity, but seemed close enough to reach out and touch.

After some years my husband needed to advance his career and we decided to go to London for him to take his master's degree. We moved to a small flat in a tall street. When I looked out of my window, I saw other flats opposite and, if I looked up, instead of a vast open sky, there was a heavy grey blanket of cloud squeezing out a permanent drizzle of rain. I set about making the flat into a comfortable home for my husband, but I was desperately homesick. One day, while shopping for lunch at the local corner store, I noticed a number of small Christmas trees for sale. I was immediately transported back to our previous Christmas, which had been spent relaxing round the pool at home, the sun beating down and the warmth enveloping me like a blanket.

Clutching my thick winter coat about me, I bought a small tree and a selection of baubles and tinsel to brighten up a corner of the flat, and took them home.

While I was decorating the tree, I had a wonderful idea. Putting the oven on as high as it would go, I took the washing-up bowl and ran down the stairs to the small garden. I filled the bowl with the thin, sour soil of London and took it back to the kitchen.

Fishing in the cupboards I found a large baking-tray, on which I spread the soil, and then put it in the oven, while I waited for my husband to come home. All day the soil baked in the oven, as I did my chores and anticipated the surprise I had in store. When I finally heard my husband's key in the lock, everything was prepared. I ran to the door to drag him into the kitchen. He watched, amazed and bemused, as I carefully took the pile of baked earth from the oven, placed it reverently on the table and then, with a flourish, sprinkled a jug of water lavishly over the tray. I wanted to create for my husband the smell of Africa after the rains come at Christmas.

Linden Green

Sick joke

To be a junior doctor in the 60s meant incredibly long hours with very little time off, and a permanent shortage of sleep. But there were compensations: we had our own mess and dining-room, and we were earning a little money after six years as impecunious medical students. We were also maturing professionally and making responsible clinical decisions. Married junior doctors were a rare species so domestic life did not encroach on our time. For a whole year the hospital was both our home and our place of work, and we only occasionally ventured into the outside world. Weekends and holidays were barely noted and Christmas was no exception.

During my year I recall the traditional Christmas dinner could not take place on Christmas Day and for various reasons we held it at the unseasonable time of late January.

The rituals, however, were not neglected and the menu, of course, included roast turkey followed by Christmas pudding, in a dining-room bedecked with holly, mistletoe, and traditional decorations. All the men put on their best suits and the women treated it as a rare opportunity to dress up. Crackers were pulled and paper hats put on. I was thoroughly enjoying the festive atmosphere, helped no doubt by a couple of sherries and a glass or two of claret, all provided generously by the senior doctors, who on this special evening stood by for emergency calls.

This was the era before 'bleeps' and we were alerted to a call by a system of three coloured lights, much like small traffic lights, strategically placed throughout the hospital. My particular set of lights was orange 'flashing' and green 'steady', a combination that for months after I had finished my house jobs still caused a momentary reflex response when out in town.

Barely had the meal started when I noticed, to my consternation, my lights were on. But I was not on call so who could want to see me? It was my ward sister informing me that a Mrs Smith was waiting in the relatives' room to see me as I had arranged (but had unfortunately forgotten). Her husband was extremely ill and as, some years previously, I had been at school with their son I was anxious to see Mrs Smith personally and inform her of the bleak outlook. Mr Smith had primary amyloid, an uncommon condition with a very poor prognosis. This was before the days of intensive care wards, artificial ventilators and renal dialysis machines. Mr Smith's disease had progressed to the stage where he was in congestive cardiac failure, renal failure and incipient respiratory failure so the interview was going to be neither easy nor pleasant. However, I thought I looked professional enough in my smart suit and if I kept my distance the traces of alcohol would not be noticed.

The interview in the small side room did not go well from the beginning. I explained the seriousness of the condition and the extremely poor prognosis. But something was wrong. The room was too hot and I didn't seem to be establishing rapport with Mrs Smith who seemed to be looking at me with a disbelieving quizzical look. Perhaps she could detect the alcohol, or perhaps I was explaining the disease and condition of her husband rather badly. Anyway, I thought the best thing to do was to finish the interview as quickly as possible, offer my sympathies and leave.

I walked away from the room still feeling uneasy with my performance and by now perspiring freely. I took my white linen handkerchief from my top pocket to mop my brow and in one ghastly moment all was explained – I still had a ridiculous paper party hat on top of my head.

Anthony Fisher